Leadership
for Students

Second Edition

Leadership for Students

A Guide for Young Leaders

Frances A. Karnes, Ph.D.
Suzanne M. Bean, Ph.D.

PRUFROCK PRESS INC.
WACO, TEXAS

Library of Congress Cataloging-in-Publication Data

Karnes, Frances A.
 Leadership for students : a guide for young leaders / Frances A. Karnes, Suzanne M. Bean. -- 2nd ed.
   p. cm.
 Includes bibliographical references.
 ISBN 978-1-59363-398-1 (pbk.)
 1. Student activities--United States. 2. Leadership--Study and teaching--United States. I. Bean, Suzanne M.,
1957- II. Title.
 LB3605.K275 2010
 303.3'4071073--dc22
                          2009032575

Copyright © 2010, Prufrock Press Inc.
Edited by Jennifer Robins
Cover and Layout Design by Marjorie Parker

ISBN-13: 978-1-59363-398-1
ISBN-10: 1-59363-398-X

Printed in the United States of America.

At the time of this book's publication, all facts and figures cited are the most current available. All telephone
numbers, addresses, and Web site URLs are accurate and active. All publications, organizations, Web sites, and
other resources exist as described in the book, and all have been verified. The authors and Prufrock Press Inc.
make no warranty or guarantee concerning the information and materials given out by organizations or content
found at Web sites, and we are not responsible for any changes that occur after this book's publication. If you
find an error, please contact Prufrock Press Inc.

Prufrock Press Inc.
P.O. Box 8813
Waco, TX 76714-8813
Phone: (800) 998-2208
Fax: (800) 240-0333
http://www.prufrock.com

TABLE OF CONTENTS

Preface vii

Introduction to Leadership 1

    Chapter 1: Defining Leadership. 15
    Chapter 2: Assessing Yourself as a Leader. 33
    Chapter 3: Opportunities for Leadership 51
    Chapter 4: Training for Leadership. 65
    Chapter 5: Influence and Encouragement From Others . . . 77
    Chapter 6: Great Leaders. .91
    Chapter 7: Advice to Others 97

Individual and Group
  Leadership Accomplishments 103

    Art for Special Hearts. 103
    A Special Wish for a Special Boy. 106
    The 13th Oak Race 108
    What Goes Around Comes Around!. 111
    One Cup at a Time!. 113

Leadership Action Journal 117

    Chapter 1 Journal Entries: Defining Leadership 119
    Chapter 2 Journal Entries: Assessing Yourself as a Leader .129
    Chapter 3 Journal Entries: Opportunities for Leadership. .145
    Chapter 4 Journal Entries: Training for Leadership 153
    Chapter 5 Journal Entries:
      Influence and Encouragement From Others 157
    Chapter 6 Journal Entries: Great Leaders 163
    Chapter 7 Journal Entries: Advice to Others. 171

Leadership Action Forms 177

Leadership Quotes. 189

Resources 197

References 213

About the Authors 215

Preface

LEADERS are needed in all segments of society—schools, communities, religious groups, business and industry, government, political groups, and the arts—and in all types of people—women, men, children, teenagers, young adults, adults, and senior citizens. Where are the great leaders in communities, states, and nations across the globe? Who are our great leaders of today? How has leadership changed? What qualities and skills are needed in leaders for the 21st century? Because of current circumstances facing our nation and world, it is clear that more serious attention should be given to developing young leaders—influential people who are critical thinkers, creative problem solvers, and strong communicators. It seems that our society has given too little time, interest, and money to developing students in the area of leadership. Just think of what we, as a nation, could accomplish if we committed ourselves to developing leadership skills and working together to make positive changes in today's world!

You most likely have many characteristics that would allow you to benefit from the development of your leadership potential. You probably have a high level of energy, a desire to make a positive difference in the world, the courage to work toward a positive goal, and the ability to solve problems creatively. With some guidance and purposeful direction, you can realize your own strengths as a leader and start putting your ideas into action! Training for leadership will help you build a positive self-concept and experience personal fulfillment. It is also a productive approach for avoiding the negative aspects of your environment. Developing habits of leadership will engage you in meaningful experiences that will help you become a responsible, influential citizen who makes the world a better place for you and all of those around you.

TARGET AUDIENCES FOR THIS BOOK

Although this book has been written for you, the student, it also will be helpful to teachers, administrators, guidance counselors, parents, and community and religious leaders. Youth leadership training is an area that can and should be the responsibility of all of these groups of people.

For teachers, school administrators, and guidance counselors, this book provides a broad-based view of leadership. It may be infused into existing curricula or it can be taught separately as specialized training in leadership. The activities in the book align with the Framework for 21st Century Learning (Partnership for 21st Century Skills, n.d.), particularly in the domains of Learning and Innovation Skills and Life and Career Skills. School personnel also may use this book in developing school clubs and Student Council groups and in planning schoolwide leadership programs and activities.

Parents often seek resources to assist them in helping their children become the best human beings they can be in hopes that they will lead happy, productive lives as they make a positive impact on the world. This is an overwhelming responsibility for parents—children's very first mentors in leadership. Parents can use the activities included in the book in the home for family discussions and learning.

Community and religious leaders who work directly with students may incorporate the activities into the framework of their organizations, too. Scouting leaders, adult civic groups, local governmental officials, members of chambers of commerce, religious personnel, and others who work with youth may use this book as a guide for understanding students' perceptions of leadership and for developing leadership experiences. Many communities across the nation now understand the importance of getting an early start to developing emerging leaders, and the activities in this book can be used toward that goal.

HOW TO USE THIS BOOK

In the Introduction to Leadership section you will find current information on how people develop as leaders, misconceptions of leadership, obstacles to leadership, and new directions and trends in leadership. There is a lot of information to process in this section but it is important for you to understand the *concept* of leadership as you develop the *skills* of leadership. You can do it!

Following that section, there are seven chapters related to defining and developing yourself as a leader. Within each chapter you will enjoy reading thoughts about leadership from others your age across the country. We initiated a national survey of youth who have participated in summer leadership development programs to find student perceptions of leadership. In these chapters, you'll notice an Ideas section and an Action section. The Ideas section includes suggestions that are taken from the responses of the youth who participated in the national survey. As you read these responses, consider how they are similar to or different from your beliefs about leadership. Discuss them with your friends or people in your group. Each Action section following student responses provides many activities for you to try. Some involve discussions with your friends, while others involve communicating through reading and writing. For those who enjoy creative projects, there are suggestions for you as well. Other activities will guide you as you bring about positive changes in your school, community, or religious organization. All of the activities outlined in the book will help you think about leadership in a serious way and become involved as you develop your own leadership potential. Select the ones that will be most helpful to you.

In the Individual and Group Leadership Accomplishments section, you will find inspiring and amazing stories of leadership in communities and schools shared by young people just like you from across the country. The Leadership Action Journal section in the second half of the book provides reproducible pages for you to record your thoughts and actions. Next, you will find the Leadership Action Forms section. These forms may be helpful with writing letters, making contacts, conducting and analyzing surveys, and developing plans for leadership. The Leadership Quotes section may inspire you and provoke you to think about leadership in many different ways. The final section, Leadership Resources, includes books, resources, organizations, and Web sites for learning more about leadership.

THANKS TO ALL

We are grateful to the many students and adults who gave of their time, effort, and expertise in the development of this project. The administration and staff at our respective universities continue to encourage and support us. A special thank you goes to Patti Davis who spent many hours typing and formatting the manuscript in preparation for publication. Jennifer Robins at Prufrock Press has been a constant source of support throughout this process, and we appreciate her commitment to the work. To our families, we thank you for your patience, love, and understanding. Words cannot express how much we love you.

Introduction
to Leadership

SHORTLY after birth, we begin on a lifelong journey of
learning about ourselves and how to interact with
other people—first our family members and later
friends, schoolmates, peers, colleagues, and business
associates. As preschool children we learn to negotiate the use
of playground equipment and make compromises over toys.
As school-aged students we test our own potential at forming
friendships and influencing others. Later in school and the
community, we join or form groups, clubs, and organizations,
and we begin to learn the art of weaving relationships as we
work with others toward common goals. This is the foundation from which leadership grows. Howard Gardner (1999)
might call these skills your *interpersonal* skills.

Also important to your leadership growth are your
intrapersonal skills. These are the skills of self-knowledge,
or understanding your own strengths, your limitations, and
areas of your personhood. In his theory of multiple intelligences, Gardner (1999) refers to these two intelligences,

interpersonal skills and intrapersonal skills, as the crowning capacity for life. Regardless of what field of study or career you choose, how well you understand yourself and how well you relate to others are skills that are critical to your success and happiness in life. Genuine leaders know themselves and connect well with others.

Others may call this *emotional intelligence.* In his book, *Emotional Intelligence: Why It Can Matter More Than IQ,* Daniel Goleman (1995) noted that people with a high level of emotional intelligence (EQ) generally are assertive people who feel positively about themselves and are able to express their feelings appropriately. These skills of emotional intelligence include, but are not limited to, putting people at ease, empathy, compassion, straightforwardness and composure, self-awareness, building and mending relationships, social poise, decision making, confronting problems and challenges, and managing change. These qualities and skills of emotional intelligence make us stronger, more human leaders.

WHY DEVELOP LEADERSHIP POTENTIAL?

Leadership begins with influence and in every person lies great potential to influence others. Some influence others in negative ways, but the most effective leaders among us are those who use their influence to move people in a positive manner toward a common purpose or goal. Whether you have a heart for helping people or you like to build relationships, there is a potential leader inside of you. You have the ability to influence others and to make positive changes in this world.

Our world is crying out for strong leaders. At a time when Americans are deeply concerned about their present and future prospects in a time of economic uncertainty and society is facing complex business, political, scientific, technological, health, and environmental challenges, strong leaders are desperately needed to guide us in hope, unity, and creative problem solving. There is greater diversity in the American population than ever before, but there also is a greater desire to experience community and collaboration.

You are part of a generation that wants to seize the moment. Youth in your generation see the mess that the world is in and feel compelled to change it. You have the potential to replace the existing pessimism with optimism and to work for the greater good of mankind. Dr. John Maxwell (2002) said, "Our world needs leaders who know the way, go the way, and show the way." You have the potential within you to accomplish this!

QUALITIES OF LEADERSHIP

In a recent article in *Parade Magazine*, renowned presidential historian Doris Kearns Goodwin (2008) identified 10 attributes of leadership that have made some of our American presidents exceptional. Although leadership does not require one to be elected into office or position, thinking about qualities of leaders seen in presidents is a good place to start. Think about what each of these qualities mean, which of them you possess, and which you would like to further develop:

- ★ the courage to stay strong,
- ★ self-confidence,
- ★ an ability to learn from errors,
- ★ a willingness to change,
- ★ emotional intelligence,
- ★ self-control,

- ★ a popular touch (awareness of what the public needs),
- ★ a moral compass,
- ★ a capacity to relax, and
- ★ a gift for inspiring others.

There are many qualities necessary for effective leaders to possess and not every leader possesses all of these qualities. It is important for you to begin to consider what you think makes a great leader and how you might begin to build some of these qualities in yourself.

PERSONALITY TYPE AND LEADERSHIP

Your personality, temperament, preferences, and talents all impact your leadership style. To learn more about your particular personality type, you might want to visit http://www.humanmetrics.com and take the Jung Typology test. It only takes a few minutes and you can learn a lot about yourself through this test. Once you know your 4-letter type, visit http://www.personalitypage.com to learn even more about your personality type and the strengths and limitations you may have as a leader. This will help build your intrapersonal skills. Remember that there is more than one right way to lead and more than one right type of leadership personality. You don't have to be an extraverted, outspoken dynamo to be an effective leader, nor do you have to fundamentally change who you are to lead. You may be a strong-willed driver; a compliant, cautious diplomat; or even a creative, sensitive dreamer. All of these personality types can contribute to leadership. The key is *knowing* yourself and *being* yourself, no matter what group you are with!

CHANGES IN LEADERSHIP

Early in the history of the world it was believed that great men (yes, at that time, men only) emerged as leaders born with certain traits or qualities that separated them from followers. Today, we know through many years of research that leadership is something that develops and grows and can be learned. Rather than the old, top-down authority ("I'm in charge") model, Lee and King (2001) offered an emerging theory of leadership that views the leader in a role of relationship and community building as multiple people work together toward a common goal. There has been a shift from autocratic to participative leadership, so collaboration, interpersonal skills, and emotional intelligence will be the keys to 21st-century leadership. The most effective leaders are those who are able to adapt and change to what is needed at that moment in time.

Leaders for the 21st century are going to need to be able to face complex challenges by being aware, paying attention, and constantly taking in new information and learning new skills. Because people in the world are looking for uniqueness and the next big thing, leaders of the 21st century will be creative thinkers and those willing to take risks. In his book *A Whole New Mind: Why Right-Brainers Will Rule the Future*, Daniel H. Pink (2006) said the future belongs to the creators, empathizers, pattern recognizers, and meaning makers. He also noted we are moving from a society built on logical, linear, computer-like capabilities of the Information Age to a society built on inventive, empathic, big-picture capabilities of what's rising in its place, the Conceptual Age. The "six senses" on which he claimed personal and professional success will depend are design, story, symphony, empathy, play, and meaning.

Powerful technologies also are changing the way leadership may work. Research from the Center for Creative Leadership (Leslie, 2003) stated that many organizations are being asked to bridge cultural, geographic, and functional boundaries, which requires skills different from face-to-face leadership. People's way of communicating may change from working face-to-face in the same office building to having a global audience and using podcasts, online communities, wikis, Twitter, Skype, and Webcams. Your generation is considered to be digital natives and you are building skills in these emerging technologies. This art of virtual leadership will not only require precision-sharp skills in changing technology but exceptionally strong written and oral communication skills as well. Are you ready for this?

MISCONCEPTIONS OF LEADERSHIP

Many confusing messages are relayed to young people in homes, schools, and communities across the nation. Often misconceptions are formed in our minds based on these messages we receive. For example, if all of the leaders in your school and community are male, you might assume, "Boys are better leaders than girls." This is a misconception that you have formed from the message you received from your environment.

Examine the list of Leadership Misconceptions and Related Facts in Table 1, and discuss them with your peers. Where do these misconceptions begin, and how are they perpetuated? How can you help to dispel these misconceptions?

TABLE 1

Leadership Misconceptions and Related Facts

Misconception	Related Facts
Boys make better leaders than girls.	Individual differences in leadership styles contribute more to effective leadership than do gender differences. Females are becoming more actively involved in leadership roles in politics, business, the arts, education, and other areas.
Think about Joan of Arc, Eleanor Roosevelt, Condoleezza Rice, and Hillary Clinton	
Firstborn children make better leaders than their later-born siblings.	The opportunities for leadership development any child experiences have more to do with his or her abilities to lead than his or her position in the family.
Think about John F. Kennedy, Donald Trump, Ted Kennedy, and Ralph Nader.	
One must be elected or appointed to be a leader.	Many nonelected or nonappointed people throughout history are now recognized as outstanding leaders in their respective fields. Many people have earned their leadership positions through hard work—not elections. There are people in your own school and community who have not been elected or appointed to leadership but who are considered leaders or "take charge" people by their friends.
Think about Mother Teresa, Benjamin Franklin, Billy Graham, and Bill Gates.	
You have to be popular to be an effective leader.	Many people throughout history have proved themselves as outstanding leaders, yet they were not popular when they began their journey as a leader. Leadership often is earned through actions, not popularity. Sometimes people in student governments or school clubs may be elected on popularity rather than leadership ability. However, they often don't get the job done!
Think about Harry Truman, Adolf Hitler, Frances Perkins, and Joseph Kony.	

Misconception	Related Facts
You can't be a leader if you live in a small, rural community.	In small schools and communities, young people have greater opportunities to participate and lead in multiple activities. Many of our great leaders of today spent most of their formative years in small, rural communities and schools.
Think about Rosa Parks, Jimmy Carter, and Bill Clinton.	
Children and young people can't really lead.	Although most of the research on leadership has looked at adult leaders, young leaders have made a significant impact on the world. People develop skills in leadership at a very early age.
Think about the students in the leadership stories in this book.	
Only people from the majority culture can be effective leaders.	People from all races and cultural backgrounds have leadership potential. People from diverse cultures may express their leadership abilities differently, but one's race or culture does not determine the level of leadership ability he or she has.
Think about Barack Obama, Barbara Jordan, Cesar Chavez, and Oprah Winfrey.	
You have to be rich to be a good leader.	One's level of wealth has nothing to do with leadership ability. Many people from poor backgrounds are highly effective leaders.
Think about Martin Luther King, Jr., Jim Thorpe, and Mary McLeod Bethune.	
You have to be outgoing to be an effective leader.	There are effective leaders who are reserved. Some may work behind the scenes, while others may lead with a more quiet style.
Think about Rachel Carson and Mohandas K. Gandhi.	
You have to make straight A's in school to be a good leader.	Superior academic ability or intelligence is not an absolute requirement for leadership. A person who works hard in school to be the best that he or she can be usually has the perseverance to be a good leader.
Think about Winston Churchill, Walt Disney, Thomas Edison, and Michael Phelps.	
Only schools offer opportunities for leadership.	Schools should offer experiences for leadership through clubs, athletics, and organizations, but opportunities for leadership also may be found in families, neighborhoods, communities, and religious affiliations.
Think about opportunities for leadership in your own community.	

Creative Problem Solving: Fuzzy Situations Regarding Leadership Misconceptions

Many young people are faced with challenges and situations that make developing into a leader seem more difficult. One of the important qualities of effective leaders is the ability to solve problems creatively and to persist through those problems to overcome them. Consider the following situations with Christina and Bob. Think about their options for solving their problems creatively. Discuss your ideas with your friends or others in your group.

Christina is a 10th-grade student at Hudson High School who is interested in developing her leadership potential. She is a member of several clubs but has never been elected as an officer. Christina is somewhat shy and has a few very close friends; however, she would not be considered one of the most popular students in school. She is particularly interested in the student government. Most of the members of the Hudson High School Student Government Association are male. In what ways might Christina develop her leadership potential?

Bob is a sixth-grade student who comes from an economically disadvantaged family background and attends school in a small community. The total population of the town is 2,462. Bob works hard in school and gets along well with young people and adults. He is interested in many areas including wildlife, the environment, drawing, and math. His greatest strength is his sense of humor. Bob wants to develop his leadership skills. In what ways might he accomplish this?

OBSTACLES TO BECOMING A LEADER

Sometimes your own personal forces and mistakes in life can interfere with your growth as a leader. For example, when you attempt a goal that is too far out of your reach at that time, you often fail to achieve the goal, which may result in a loss of self-confidence. A lack of self-confidence is an obstacle to leadership development. These and other obstacles can be overcome through recognition of them and consistent efforts to improve in these areas.

Look at Table 2, Obstacles to Becoming a Leader and Alternatives Toward Leadership Development. What are other obstacles you have experienced in your pursuit of leadership potential? What alternatives have you found successful in overcoming these obstacles?

Another major obstacle to becoming a leader is a lack of time management. Effective leaders must be in charge of their own time and must organize and work around priorities. Managing your time effectively determines the quality of your leadership.

Many young people aspiring toward leadership find this obstacle to be a most difficult one to master. It is often very easy to put things off until the last minute or to choose only the fun or easy activities to do, but procrastination is a significant hindrance to productive leadership. The results of procrastination can restrict leadership development and personal growth.

Analyze the Time Management Matrix in Table 3 and assess your own ability in this area. What are the activities that keep you from being as productive as you could be? How do you spend most of your free time? How can you make better use of your time?

Leadership for Students

TABLE 2

Obstacles to Becoming a Leader and Alternatives Toward Leadership Development

Lack of Self-Confidence
Engage yourself in activities that help build your confidence and surround yourself with people who encourage your abilities.

Negative Attitudes
- ★ "There's nothing I can do about it."
- ★ "That's just the way I am."
- ★ "I'm sure they won't allow us to do that."

Work on developing an "I can" attitude or at least an "I'll try" attitude. Effective leaders have positive attitudes!

Extreme Shyness
Try getting involved in activities that include a few other people rather than large groups. This may help you to become more comfortable with others, and you can gradually work up to larger groups.

Inability to Listen to Others
Learn to keep your mouth closed more and your ears and mind open to others' ideas.

Not Setting Priorities
Choose activities that are most important to you. Someone who tries to do everything may find that he or she is not really effective at anything.

Not Setting Goals
When priorities have been determined, set your goals toward completion of activities or projects. How will you know where you are going if you don't choose a path to follow?

Wanting and Trying to Do It All Yourself
Some people strive for power and recognition rather than real leadership. You must realize that an effective leader is also a team player. Work hard to make sure all members of the group are actively involved and are recognized for their contributions.

Lack of Perseverance
Some people start many projects but have a difficult time finishing them. This usually means they lack "stick-to-it-ive-ness." Effective leaders must not give up on projects they start no matter how difficult or time consuming they may be.

TABLE 3

Time Management Matrix

Procrastinators . . .	Effective Time Managers . . .
★ are unorganized. ★ welcome and accept interruptions. ★ work on insignificant activities. ★ daydream. ★ try to take on too many activities. ★ talk rather than do. ★ don't make choices or choose fun activities only. ★ put things off until the deadline arrives. ★ are reactive.	★ set priorities. ★ eliminate unnecessary activities. ★ set goals. ★ get organized. ★ use calendars or appointment books. ★ make and use lists. ★ engage in daily planning. ★ make choices. ★ are proactive. ★ delegate tasks to others.
Results	
Procrastinators . . .	Effective Time Managers . . .
★ have stress. ★ burn out. ★ feel out of control. ★ break promises. ★ suffer a decrease in self-esteem. ★ lose respect for others. ★ are irresponsible. ★ depend on others.	★ have discipline. ★ have control. ★ have balance. ★ are productive. ★ are self-reliant. ★ increase their self-esteem. ★ have respect for others. ★ are responsible. ★ obtain leadership positions.

Moral and Ethical Dimensions of Leadership

Leadership with ethics leads to service to humanity. To what does leadership without ethics lead? Can someone be an effective leader without acceptable moral or ethical standards? How about Hitler? Sometimes leadership ability is channeled in a negative direction resulting in manipulation and corruption. For example, a gang leader may have strong leadership ability, but sometimes uses this ability in a destructive way. Too often we focus on the mechanics of leadership, and we neglect one of the most important dimensions—the heart of leadership—morality and ethics.

Examine the Moral and Ethical Dimensions of Leadership found in Table 4. Does power corrupt? How are acceptable moral and ethical standards set? What determines a morally mature leader? Are there leaders who have had unethical causes, but moral actions? Are there leaders who have had moral causes, but unethical actions? What is your plan for your own growth toward becoming an ethical leader?

FINAL THOUGHTS

When we really analyze the concept of leadership, we find that there are many new dimensions to be explored. It is important to continue your study of the concept of leadership and to study yourself, other people, and the ever-changing world around you. Remember that leadership develops *daily*, not in a day, a week, a month, or a year. It is a journey. It is a process. Even the oldest, wisest, most effective leader alive today is continually learning. By reading this book you have committed to preparing yourself for a life of leadership and service to others and you should be commended for that. Now get busy—your school, community, nation, and world need you!

TABLE 4

Moral and Ethical Dimensions of Leadership

Leaders Who Lack Morality or Ethics May . . .	Morally Acceptable Leaders . . .
★ be cruel to their own group members.	★ serve the common good and at the same time pay attention to individual interests.
★ treat followers well, but encourage them to do evil things to others.	★ transmit a sense of mission.
★ use followers' weaknesses like fear, paranoia, hate, bigotry, or desire for revenge.	★ encourage followers to go beyond their own self-interests.
★ manipulate group members.	★ promote harmony.
★ diminish their followers, making them dependent and childlike.	★ demonstrate integrity.
★ believe that the end justifies the means.	★ are compassionate and sensitive to the needs of others.
★ distort reality and use propaganda.	★ are authentic.
★ set group members against one another.	★ resolve conflicts fairly.
★ use intimidation, threats, bribery, and coercion to motivate.	★ share in the leadership tasks.
★ be self-serving and egocentric.	★ work toward releasing human possibilities.
★ lack sensitivity to others' needs.	★ foster individual initiative, but expect a certain amount of initiative to be expended on shared purposes.
★ be dominated by group values or peer pressure.	★ are tolerant and hold mutual respect for others.
★ lack their own set of values, standards, and ideals.	★ enrich commitment to freedom, justice, equality of opportunity, and dignity and worth of the individual.
Historical Examples of Leaders Who Lacked Morality or Ethics	**Historical Examples of Morally Acceptable Leaders**
★ Adolf Hitler	★ Rachel Carson
★ Idi Amin	★ Mohandas Gandhi
★ Joseph Stalin	★ Martin Luther King, Jr.
★ Ayatollah Khomeini	★ George Washington
★ James Jones	★ Indira Gandhi
★ Joseph Kony	★ Mother Teresa

Defining Leadership

What Is Leadership?

Our survey found that although some elementary age students referred to leadership as power, authority, and control, the majority of students defined leadership in positive terms. The responses reflect a wide range of characteristics and behaviors of leadership. In general, the older students identified leadership as a multidimensional concept.

Ideas

Leadership is being part of a team, not just the leader of a group. You are not a leader if no one is following.
Male, 16

A leader is a person who helps others, learns different skills, and develops the character to live a life of excellence.
Female, 13

Leadership is the desire and ability to guide, direct, and lead others to do things for others and themselves.
Female, 13

Leadership is the ability to influence others to complete a specific task.
Female, 16

Leadership is when you motivate others by example, word of mouth, and influence. It also includes bringing out the full potential in someone.
Male, 14

Leadership is possessing a quality that your peers can follow.
Male, 16

Leadership is knowing how to lead a number of people. To have leadership, you must possess integrity, honesty, and determination.
Female, 14

Leaders create opportunities to help others and guide others to be the best they can be.

Male, 13

Leadership is the act, concept, or behavior of a leader. Leadership is also the capability to guide, inspire, or direct others.

Female, 12

Leadership is when a person is perceived to be powerful and takes charge.

Female, 12

Leadership is influencing or helping others to accomplish a mission or a goal.

Female, 9

Actions

Think About It

★ Which one of the definitions of leadership listed above do you like best? Why?

★ What is your definition of leadership?

★ Survey your friends to get their ideas on definitions of leadership.

★ What is the definition of leadership in the dictionary? Compare and contrast it to those given by the students above. Compare and contrast it to your definition of leadership.

★ Think of three famous leaders (e.g., political, religious, social). What do you think their definitions of leadership would be? How would their definitions be alike? How would they be different?

★ How do you think leadership will be different when you are an adult? How will you prepare for this?

★ Choose three leaders from different areas and research them. Perhaps you will choose a religious, political, social, or business leader, or one in the arts, humanities, or sports. Which one appeals most to you? Analyze his or her responsibilities.

★ Name students you know who fit your definition of leadership. What qualities of theirs would you like to develop or enhance in yourself?

Talk About It

★ Think of your three favorite movies. Which ones have an element of leadership within the story? Discuss this with your friends.

★ Who among your friends is the most influential? Why is that so?

Write About It

★ Write a short story, poem, essay, rap, or song based on your definition of leadership.

★ What will be the definition of leadership in the next century?

★ Write a story on leadership for your school newspaper.

Do It

★ What information can you find on leadership? Google the term "leadership." Do you agree or disagree with the information you find? If you disagree with the information, write what you think should be written about leadership and include it in your journal or send it to your local newspaper for possible publication.

★ Make a poster or visual display of what leadership is or means to you. Include words, pictures, and anything else that visually represents the concept of leadership. Hang it in your room as inspiration or ask your principal to hang it in your school. Ask if your principal or art teacher would sponsor a school art contest with a leadership theme.

★ Make a bumper sticker that conceptualizes leadership. Ask a club in your school or community to have it made and sold to raise funds for a leadership training program for youth.

★ Some people think of leadership as being the same as popularity. What do you think? Conduct a debate or panel discussion with some of your friends or classmates on this topic.

★ Ask five leaders in your school to talk to your class or club about what they think leadership is and compare and contrast their responses.

★ Look at leadership in a new way. What is the color of leadership? What is the smell of leadership? If you could touch leadership, how would it feel? Use your responses to these questions to make a sculpture or some other visual display of leadership and display it in your school or community.

★ How is leadership connected to other disciplines and components of society? Using the web on page 123 as a guide, create a model or a diagram of connections with leadership.

What Are the Most Important Characteristics Needed to Be a Leader?

Our survey showed that students identify a wide variety of characteristics of a leader; however, several characteristics emerged as the most frequently cited. Those characteristics were communication, responsibility, self-confidence, intelligence, and decision-making skills. Other responses not cited as frequently, but important to leadership, were perception, control of emotions, a strong sense of morality, and the ability to take a risk. The responses indicated that the students were well-informed of the characteristics of leaders.

Ideas

Passion for your particular activity, vision to accomplish your goal and to make it better, inspiration for the project so you never forget the reason or who you are doing it for.
Female, 17

Showing your team that you will not ask them to do anything you would not do yourself. Also, a leader is not being too high and mighty to do a job with your team if they need you.
Male, 16

To show the way for others, and to take control of affairs or actions.

Female, 13

The most important characteristics of being a leader are to have excellent communication skills, to be open-minded, to be able to set goals and accomplish them in a timely manner.

Female, 16

Honesty, courage, responsibility, social skills, optimism, integrity, and intelligence.

Male, 14

The most important characteristics for being a leader are citizenship, service, scholarship, and character as well as the desire to inspire others. A good sense of humor should be also part of a great leader's character.

Female, 13

Charisma, having a calm attitude, being passionate about your beliefs, and having sound judgment.

Male, 16

The most important characteristics for being a leader are integrity, honesty, determination, and the willingness to lead.

Female, 14

Willing to give of yourself, being loyal to others, and being trustworthy.

Male, 13

The most important characteristics of being a leader are being motivational, valiant, enlightening, passionate, and broadminded.

Female, 12

The most important characteristics of being a leader are being empathetic, sympathetic, fearless, passionate, and wise.

Female, 12

Assertiveness; respectful; democratic; motivator; persuasive; flexibility; communicator; and goal-oriented.

Female, 9

Actions

Think About It

★ Are there other important characteristics of leadership that were not mentioned above?

★ List characteristics of leadership that you think are important and rate yourself on these characteristics.

★ How will you develop your weak areas?

★ Think of one female and one male leader. List and compare and contrast the leadership characteristics of each. What are the similarities? The differences?

Read About It

★ Read several articles or books on great leaders and make a chart with their leadership characteristics.

Write About It

★ After reading about leaders, write a short essay about the characteristics of your favorite leaders. Describe both the positive and negative characteristics of each leader from the above stories.

★ Which characteristics do you have?

★ Name a characteristic of leadership for each letter of the alphabet.

★ Brainstorm characteristics of leadership. Group your responses according to those characteristics that you believe people are born with and those characteristics that people must learn.

Do It

★ Conduct a survey by asking your friends what they believe to be the most important characteristics for being a good leader. Make a chart showing the results and post it in your classroom or in the hall in your school. Be sure to get permission before doing so.

★ Investigate the research that has been conducted on the differences in male and female leadership characteristics. Create a play or short drama enacting the male and female styles of leadership. Make projections as to how you think the shift in leadership characteristics and styles will change society. Debate this topic with friends.

★ Create a cartoon character that has all of the characteristics of leadership that you think are important. Write a story about that character and his or her ideas about leadership. Share the story with younger students.

What Are the Positive Aspects of Being a Leader?

The nature of the students' responses to this question indicated that the majority of students have experienced a leadership position. The most frequently cited positive aspects of being a leader were helping others, the sense of being needed, belonging to a group, the feeling of accomplishment upon achievement of a goal, self-growth and understanding, and gaining the respect of others.

Ideas

The benefits of leadership for women are the sense of accomplishment one gets from volunteering, the effect of helping in the community and the value one feels when working with other women.
Female, 17

Watching your team grow and giving them the skills and the knowledge to become leaders themselves.
Male, 16

The positive benefits of being a leader are good communications with others, understanding, and patience.
Female, 13

A benefit of being a leader is creating a sense of unity in a group.
> *Male, 16*

One of the positive aspects of being a leader is the fact that a great leader can inspire and enable each and every one in his or her group to reach their full potential.
> *Female, 13*

One positive aspect of being a leader is having that feeling of accomplishment. To know that you may have changed somebody's life for the better. A leader must be able to guide others.
> *Female, 16*

People look up to you as being a role model. You can be bad or you can be good. You will be the one people come to when they have a problem in their life.
> *Male, 14*

The positive aspects are that you become a respectable, responsible, and admired person. People will always follow as you lead.
> *Female, 14*

Helping others to complete a task, seeing success in others, sharing your knowledge with others.
> *Male, 13*

The positive aspects of being a leader are having great supporters, gaining respect, and having the ability to influence others to be leaders.

Female, 12

The positive aspects include feeling a great sense of accomplishment when a task is completed successfully.

Female, 9

The positive aspects of being a leader are that you have a chance to make a difference; you have the opportunity to show the world a different point of view and make people listen and understand what you are.

Female, 12

Actions

Think About It

* Review the responses given by the students and select the ones that would be like yours and state why.
* How do you think Barack Obama, Mahatma Gandhi, Martin Luther King, Jr., Hillary Clinton, or Eleanor Roosevelt would respond to the same question?

Write About It

* Make your own list of the positive aspects of being a leader. Keep them in your leadership journal or post them in your room so that you can keep focused on them.

Talk About It

★ Interview your school principal and counselor and ask them about the positive aspects of their leadership positions and their ideas on effective leadership. Design a way to let students know the results.

Do It

★ Think of leaders in the categories of religion, arts, science, government, politics, and the like. Contact one in each category and ask for a statement from each on the positive aspects of being a leader from their perspective. Develop a display to share with your friends and other students.

★ Write a skit for younger children that shows the positive aspects of being a leader. Present the skit to a group of younger children in your school, community, or religious organization.

★ Examine the changes that have occurred in leadership since the beginning of time. Design a docudrama of this historical perspective of leadership and focus on the positive aspects of being a leader in today's society. Videotape it and post it on YouTube.

★ Design a poster or visual representation of real-life leaders and what each would say are the positive aspects of leadership.

★ Interview student leaders in your school, community, or religious organization and ask them to define the positive aspects of being a leader. Compare the responses that were given. Do those leaders have the same ideas about positive aspects of leadership? How are their responses different according to their positions of leadership? Compare your own responses to those given. Design a graph (e.g., pie chart, bar graph) on your computer using the results and post it on your school's Web site. Be sure to ask permission before doing so.

> ## What Are the Negative Aspects of Being a Leader?

Our survey revealed that the majority of responses have to do with the way other people may respond to someone in a leadership position. Specific reactions from others that the students identified as negative were hate, jealousy, loss of faith, criticism, blame, and rejection. Other negative aspects of leadership cited included stress, pressure, the lack of privacy, the possibility of making a mistake, and the amount of time required of someone in a leadership position.

Ideas

For me, I am the primary (and actual sole) person responsible for the monthly project—organizing and developing craft ideas, buying supplies, performing the activity, and recruiting volunteers. It's a lot of work.
Female, 17

One of the negative aspects of being a leader would be the fact that, regardless how hard one tries to enable and inspire others, failure is always a possibility.

Female, 13

Sometimes you have to work with people who aren't willing to compromise and you may end up trying to accomplish a goal by yourself and that can be tiring.

Female, 16

You are watched constantly, so when you do something wrong, you might have a negative influence on someone. If you lead someone down a wrong path, it could mess up their whole lives.

Male, 14

Sometimes when you are in the position of a leader, it gets taken too far. You might start to do more than is needed sometimes. Also, you might react in a way that's not expected.

Female, 14

Some people may not understand you. You may have to answer a lot of questions about why you don't do things others do.

Male, 13

The negative aspects of being a leader are having doubters of your abilities and being put under pressure.

Female, 12

The overall ability of a group to be open-minded is limited and this may be frustrating to a leader.
> *Male, 16*

The negative aspects of being a leader are that a group of people will blame the leader when a mistake is made.
> *Female, 12*

Sometimes being a leader puts a lot of pressure on me when others are depending on me to do everything well.
> *Female, 9*

Actions

Think About It

★ What do you believe to be or what have you experienced as the negative aspects of leadership?

★ What would you say to a friend who only thinks of the negative side of leadership?

★ As a leader, how would you deal with criticism, jealousy, unrealistic expectations, loss of personal time, and pressures?

★ How would you handle a situation in which you, as the leader, were unjustly blamed for the failure of a project?

★ Imagine that you are an important leader of a big group. What would you like to say to your followers that may prevent negative attitudes?

Read About It

★ Read about the life of a famous leader and list what he or she might consider to be the negative aspects of leadership. How did this leader deal with the negative parts of leadership?

Do It

★ Organize a debate on the positive and negative sides of leadership.

★ How would you convince other young people that developing leadership skills can be very positive for them personally and professionally?

★ Develop a plan of action for this goal and put it to work.

★ As a leader, how would you deal with or overcome the part of leadership that you think is negative? List the negative aspects of leadership and ways you could turn them into positives.

★ Interview leaders in your school or community and ask what they think the negative aspects are and how they deal with them.

★ Prepare a speech or a paper on topics such as "The Positive and Negative Aspects of Leadership" or "How to Turn the Negatives of Leadership Into Positives." Present it to an appropriate group of students.

Assessing Yourself as a Leader

How Do You Know That You Are a Leader?

Our survey found that all of the students responding to this question do believe that they are leaders. Some students stated that they know they are leaders because of the way others treat them with respect and as role models. Other students cited personal qualities as indicators of their ability to lead such as comfort in leadership positions, being a trendsetter, persuasiveness, the ability to withstand peer pressure, and the ability to take charge.

Ideas

It seems natural to me to see what needs to be done and do it!

Female, 17

By the respect and the accomplishments of your team.

Male, 16

I do what I'm told to the best of my ability. I'm easy to get along with and like working with others. I like showing others the best way of doing things.

Female, 13

Knowing that you are a great leader shows in your actions. If taking charge of situations, guiding others, overcoming obstacles, and facing responsibility for your actions comes naturally to you, chances are you have leadership skills.

Female, 13

I know that I'm a leader because I have this way of motivating people who would normally not do work. I also know I'm a leader because my classmates are always looking to me for help with work or anything else. Some of them won't work until they ask me what to do.

Female, 16

I am looked up to by younger peers. Whenever they have a situation they need help with they ask me for advice.

Male, 14

When you can see your peers follow you loyally.
Male, 16

I am able to take charge of a group in a respectful manner in order to delegate tasks, recruit others to help out, and to take risks in order to accomplish a task.
Female, 9

You know you are a leader when people look up to you and follow your lead. People will watch what you do closely, and you will try to make a good impression of yourself all the time.
Female, 14

I know I'm a leader because I make good decisions, enjoy helping others, and enjoy working with people.
Male, 13

I know I am a leader because I am very respectful and listen to others' opinions. I am a positive person and have plenty of self-confidence. I also understand how to get to the top. I know when to stake my grounds and be a leader as well as when to sit down and be a follower. In other words, I realize that you have to learn before you can teach.
Female, 12

You know you are a leader when you stand up and fight for what you believe in; even though you may be small you are still passionate about your belief and ready to lead.
Female, 12

Think About It

* Which responses of the students would be similar to yours? Why is it important for a good leader to also be a good follower?
* Which responses are different? Why?
* What are the characteristics of a good follower?
* How would you rate yourself on knowing when to follow and being a good follower? How could you improve your skills in following others when needed?

Write About It

* Prepare a campaign speech about your abilities as a leader that you might use if you were running for office.
* List the ways that you have been a leader either formally or informally.
* List the ways that you have been a leader in your school, community, or religious organization. Circle the leadership roles that you have enjoyed the most. Write down the reasons why you liked the roles that you circled and the reasons why you didn't like the others.
* Keep a log or a diary for a year and record all of the ways you were a leader.
* Make a list of all of the extracurricular activities in which you are involved (e.g., clubs, athletics, organizations, hobbies). Analyze your role in these groups. Do you usually take charge of activities? Do you usually wait for someone else to tell you what to do?

* How do you see yourself as a leader in the future? Write a scenario of your life as a leader 15 years from now. Write a description of the types of leadership experience you will have, the ideas to be conveyed, the leadership style you will use, and the feelings you have about leadership.

Do It

* Using your computer, draw a picture or make a collage of how you see yourself as a leader during the coming year. Post it on your personal Web site or on a social networking site if you are a member (e.g., Facebook, MySpace).
* Make a list of other extracurricular activities in which you would like to be involved. Come up with strategies for getting involved in these activities.
* Think of one or two people whom you consider to be leaders. Make a list of characteristics or behaviors that these people possess. Rate yourself 1–5 on each of these items (1 being low and 5 being high). What can you do to continue building on your leadership strengths? Develop a strategy for working on your weaker areas. You may want to get advice from adult leaders in your community.
* Initiate a "Leader of the Month" program in your school or community. This would give recognition to the young person who has shown leadership ability over a given time period. Ask for support for this proposal from the local Chamber of Commerce, community groups, and adult leaders.

What Is Your Attitude Toward Being a Leader?

Our survey found that students regarded leadership with pride, honor, and a degree of seriousness. They also stated that being a leader is fun, challenging, and very rewarding. Some students felt that leadership should be a shared responsibility because too much leadership from one person can result in a negative situation.

Ideas

Although I am capable of following directions from others, I usually have strong feelings about how something needs to be done and can see the final result.
Female, 17

My attitude is positive and I like to keep my team on a positive note.
Male, 16

My attitude toward being a leader is to analyze, research, and strategize.
Female, 13

I have a positive attitude towards being a leader. I think that if you are a good person headed in the right direction, you can change the world.

Female, 16

I take it for what it's worth, nothing more or less. I would want to lead like an Abraham or Martin Luther King. I would prefer to be looked at as a positive influence on anyone who's around me.

Male, 14

I feel proud to be a leader because it makes me feel that I am helping others.

Female, 9

It helps to accomplish things in an efficient manner and maintain unity.

Male, 16

I think that being a leader is a great thing to be. It is something that I strive for all the time. I want people to think of me as someone who leads and doesn't follow. That always is a good thing.

Female, 14

Being a good leader is important because you are helping others to do the right thing.

Male, 13

My attitude toward being a leader is very jubilant. I have an optimistic approach to both good and bad outcomes. In my opinion, a positive thinker receives positive results.
Female, 12

My attitude toward being a leader is that it can be a rewarding, fun experience.
Female, 12

Actions

Think About It

★ Which student above do you think has the best attitude toward being a leader? Which attitude is most like yours? Least like yours?

Write About It

★ Write a short essay, poem, or rap about your attitude toward being a leader.

★ Do you think political leaders' attitudes toward leadership affect your attitudes? Are political leaders' attitudes toward leadership changing? If so, do you believe their attitudes are changing in a negative or positive way? Contact local, state, and federal politicians for their responses to these questions. Write a statement about this and share it with your friends.

Do It

★ Conduct and analyze a survey of your school class regarding students' attitudes about being a leader. Ask the editor of your school newspaper if the paper can publish the results of your survey or publish the results on your school Web site. Be sure to get permission first!

★ Ask your parents about their attitudes toward your desire to be a leader. Do you agree with what they said? Why or why not?

★ What are the attitudes toward leadership of students your age from other parts of the country or from foreign countries? Locate three pen pals from different countries and e-mail them! Ask them how they feel about leadership. Then, write a short piece on attitudes about leadership in other countries and how these compare to attitudes found in the United States. Think of a creative way to share this with others online.

★ Complete the following statement: I think leadership is important because . . .

★ Conduct a survey in your school or community to determine differences (if any) in male and female attitudes toward leadership. What impact do you think these differences may have on society in the future?

★ Ask leaders in your town about their attitudes toward being leaders. How are their attitudes toward leadership alike and how are they different?

★ What do you think your teacher's attitude is about you being a leader? Ask! Were you correct?

★ What do you think the attitudes of the presidents of large companies are toward being leaders? Contact them to ask. Were you correct?

What Is Your Strongest Area of Leadership Skill?

Our survey indicated that the responses can be grouped into three major categories: people-oriented skills, task-oriented skills, and qualities or attributes of leadership. The statements that were more people-oriented were, for the most part, interpersonal skills such as working with others, communicating, and motivating people. The task-oriented category consists of responses such as solving problems, thinking logically, finding information, and organizing plans. The qualities of leadership cited as strengths were foresight, innovativeness, confidence, persistence, and persuasiveness.

Ideas

Insight—I can see the final result and am willing to do what is required to get there.
Female, 17

I feel my strongest area would be keeping the workers positive and feeling good about themselves and what they are doing.
Male, 16

By being willing to do anything it takes no matter how hard the tasks are.
Female, 13

My strongest leadership skill is that I am able to lead as well as follow.

Female, 13

My strongest area of leadership skill is that I am fearless and have good public speaking skills.

Female, 12

My strongest area of leadership skill is making decisions and helping others to make decisions that are right for them.

Female, 16

I am a very outspoken person. I am not shy. I give good advice on most subjects.

Male, 14

Persuasion is my strongest area of leadership because I am able to present ideas in such a way that makes others become excited about them.

Female, 9

Sound judgment.

Male, 16

I am someone who can connect with people easily, and I think that is a leadership skill that helps me out greatly.

Female, 14

Meeting people and talking to them.

Male, 13

My strongest area of leadership skill is my self-motivation.
I have the ability to push myself and find a necessary
reason to have strength without the need of being
influenced by others.

Female, 12

Actions

Think About It

★ How will you use your strengths to be a leader?

★ What are the strengths of the leaders in your school or community?

★ Think of your three strongest areas of leadership skills. How might you encourage someone to develop him- or herself in these areas?

Write About It

★ Write a speech nominating yourself for the "Great Leaders' Hall of Fame." Include your areas of strength in leadership.

★ Write a speech to get elected to a position of your choice in your school or community.

Do It

★ List all of your strengths in leadership skills. Put them in order from the strongest to the weakest. How do you plan to increase the skills that you consider the weakest? Select a leader whom you admire and list his or her strongest areas of leadership and compare both lists. How are they alike and how are they different?

- ★ Collect biographical information on three famous leaders. Analyze the information to determine the strengths of each leader. Compare and contrast these strengths their strengths with your own.
- ★ Using your computer, design a personal leadership logo for yourself incorporating your leadership strengths. Post it on your personal Web site or on a social networking site if you are a member (e.g., Facebook, MySpace).
- ★ Keeping leadership strengths in mind, comprise an analogy comparing leadership to some nonhuman item. For example, "A leader is like a sponge because he or she can absorb a great deal of information and put it to good use for the benefit of others," or "A leader is like a lion because it has gained respect of all other animals through its strength."

Our survey found that many students saw their weakest areas in skills such as decision making, organization, oral and written communication, and delegating. Others spoke of personal characteristics that often kept them from being effective leaders such as procrastination, lack of aggressiveness, inability to accept criticism, lack of patience, inability to admit mistakes, lack of control over emotions, too much concern with trying to please everyone, and too much sensitivity. The responses, in general, showed that the students were very aware of their deficiencies regarding skills necessary for the process of leadership.

Ideas

My weakest area of leadership skill is that I do not like to share my personal zone. I am working on a balance.
Female, 12

Time management.
Female, 17

Trying to do it all myself. It's been hard learning that I can't do it all by myself.
Male 16

Trying to help kids that don't want to learn, I get impatient.
Female, 13

My weakest leadership skill is the fact that I don't accept failure; quitting in any situation at any given point is hard for me, therefore accepting failure is my weakest leadership skill.
Female, 13

Charisma.
Male, 16

My weakest area of leadership is trying to keep and make everyone happy.
Female, 16

I have a problem with taking charge. I don't like to hurt people in any form or fashion. I also have a problem with listening to criticism.

Male, 14

My weakest area is staying focused. I will know what I need to do, and sometimes little things distract me from the thing at hand.

Female, 14

I have a hard time giving up control and letting others contribute to projects.

Female, 9

Telling people they have done something wrong.

Male, 13

My weakest area of leadership skill is control. I am the kind of person who desires to take notice of everyone's point of view so sometimes it is hard for me to come up with a conclusion that everyone will agree with.

Female, 12

Actions

Think About It

★ Is your weakest area the same as any of those given above? If not, what is it?

★ What do you think are or were the weakest areas of leadership for George W. Bush, Dick Cheney, Franklin

Delano Roosevelt, Amelia Earhart, Jonas Salk, and John Glenn? How did they overcome these weak areas?

★ Select a leader you would like to emulate. How will you have to change in order to do this?

Talk About It

★ Identify and talk with someone in your school or community to help you improve your weakest leadership skills. Find someone who knows you well and will be honest with you.

★ Think of a friend who lacks leadership ability. Plan ways you could help him or her to develop his or her leadership abilities. Can you discuss this with your friend? Be sure to ask him or her for advice on how to improve your own leadership abilities as well.

★ Interview school, community, or state leaders about what their initial weaknesses were and how they overcame or improved these weaknesses as a leader. Summarize your findings and share it with others in a creative way. You may want to keep the responses anonymous.

★ Get a group of three or four of your friends together and have each person list three strengths and three weaknesses (in terms of leadership abilities) for each person in the group. Swap lists so that each person has his or her own lists of strengths and weaknesses. Discuss them with your friends if you feel comfortable with this.

Write About It

★ Keep a diary or log of particularly weak areas of leadership you would like to strengthen. Make a record of your behavior and actions as you work toward improving them.

- ★ Think about three weak areas of leadership that you would like to work on. Develop strategies for improving your weak areas.

Do It

- ★ What will you do about your weakest areas? Develop a plan to turn your weakest areas into strengths. Write your goal, objectives, activities, potential resource person(s), and a timeline for completing this.
- ★ What other areas would you like to strengthen? Develop additional plans.
- ★ Write a comedy skit on how one must overcome weaknesses in leadership. Get your friends to join you and present it to your class or videotape it and post it on YouTube.
- ★ Draw a cartoon strip showing what could happen to weak leaders.
- ★ Make a list of the changes that you would like to make in your leadership abilities. Design a progress chart that you will follow for the next week, month, or year.
- ★ Role-play situations in which leaders must be assertive. Identify assertive behaviors that you would like to have and practice them.
- ★ Role-play a situation in which you as a leader must admit a mistake to the group.
- ★ Think of ways to convince your friends or classmates to successfully complete a project and try them out.
- ★ Make a list of your weaknesses as a leader. For each area you consider to be a weakness, determine two or three strategies for improving in those areas. Ask an adult who is close to you to look at your ideas and discuss them with you.

Opportunities
for Leadership

What Opportunities
Do You Have for
Being a Leader in
Your School?

Our survey found that the majority of students saw many opportunities for being a leader in their schools. Opportunities included those associated with Student Councils, sports, fine and performing arts, and academics. A few students gave examples for opportunities for leadership within the classroom.

Ideas

Opportunities are great but I feel like I wanted to devote my time and energy to what I am passionate about— helping others, especially the mentally disabled, who are less fortunate.

Female, 17

I can be a leader in the classroom. As I get older, I can be a leader in clubs and organizations.

Female, 9

Being in the Key Club, being a part of the baseball team, and being a student.

Male, 16

I have an opportunity to be in Beta Club, Student Council, and office helper.

Female, 13

By being an active athlete in my school I have multiple opportunities to show my leadership skills on the field, in the locker room, as well as in practices. Also, by being vice president for our school's National Junior Honor Society I have to show my leadership on a daily basis.

Female, 13

Opportunities are limited at my school for being a leader. However, some opportunities are being in JROTC, having a high GPA, and being a good student.

Female, 16

I am a member of the basketball team and I am running for Student Council. I can tutor during the lifeboat outreach program.
Male, 14

At the middle school I have a chance to be part of the Student Council and a part of the Technology Parent/ Teacher group.
Female, 12

Basketball team and Student Council.
Male, 16

The opportunities at my school are being a class officer, serving as an officer of a club, or just leading in the classroom.
Female, 14

Being a good friend, and making the right decisions even if your friends do not agree.
Male, 13

The opportunities I have for being a leader at my school are the diverse clubs and organizations my school provides, such as: The National Beta Club, Honor's Society, Global Technology Association, and the Student Council of each grade. My school also has an afterschool remediation program where students are permitted to voluntarily aid other students.
Female, 12

Think About It

★ What other opportunities for being a leader in your school would you like to have? How could you help develop more opportunities?

★ Some people believe that leaders are chosen because they are popular. What do you think? Are your school leaders only leaders because they are popular? If so, what could be done to change the system so that those with the most leadership ability would be elected instead?

★ What is the difference between an elected leader and a leader who emerges in a group activity? In what ways could you be a leader in your school other than being elected or appointed?

Write About It

★ Write an article for the school newspaper or prepare a speech about the opportunities for being a leader in your school.

Do It

★ Hold a meeting for other students who might like to have additional opportunities for leadership in the school. As a group, write a brief proposal outlining why you would like more opportunities for leadership and give examples of additional opportunities you would like to have incorporated in your school. Arrange for a meeting with interested parents, school board members, administrators, counselors, and teachers to present your proposal.

* Give your school principal a "Recipe for Leadership." The recipe should include a step-by-step approach to developing the leadership of students in your school.

* Using past school yearbooks or other printed material that may be available through your principal, create a historical diagram of the clubs, organizations, and other opportunities for leadership that have been offered in your school since it began. How have these opportunities changed? Are there more or fewer opportunities now? Analyze the progression of these opportunities in your school and write a brief report to present to your principal, faculty, or school board.

* Design a survey to send to friends and relatives who attend schools other than yours. Ask that they list all opportunities for leadership in their school and return the form to you. Make a composite list of potential leadership opportunities in your school and compare and contrast it to the list of opportunities you have received from other schools. How are they alike? How are they different? Are there opportunities for leadership in other schools that could be used in your school?

* Analyze the responsibilities of the presidents of all of the clubs and organizations in your school. Do they all have the same duties? Which presidents are the most effective? How can the others become more effective?

* Make a list of all of the scholastic and sports leadership positions in your school and responsibilities of each. Circle the ones that are most important to you. Develop step-by-step guide for yourself for being a leader in your school.

* Complete the following statement: I want to be a leader in my school because . . .

★ Brainstorm a list of elected positions in school and ways that a person can be a leader in school without being elected.

Our survey found that students gave many examples of opportunities for being a leader in their community such as organized youth clubs and associations, community projects, and their jobs. A few students were able to develop their own, self-initiated opportunities for leadership by developing new clubs and organizations within their communities.

Ideas

Opportunities are endless if you are willing to do the work.
Female, 17

I am a leader on the soccer field, softball field, and basketball court during community sports.
Female, 9

Through the Key Club and through my church.
Male, 16

In my community I work at the local soup kitchen. At times I represent at local special events and convey information from the Technology Parent/Teacher group.
Female, 12

Being involved in ministries. Getting involved with Girl Scouts or church functions and also getting involved with recreation activities.
Female, 13

I have many opportunities to show leadership in my community by organizing clean-ups, food and clothes drives, and raising awareness on current problems.
Female, 13

There are organizations such as the Mayor's Youth Council of which I am the vice president. This organization allows young people to experience new things.
Female, 16

I can go to the nursing home and give them my company. This includes reading to them, playing board games, and maybe even bringing an occasional gift.
Male, 14

The opportunities I have for being a leader in my community are the Mayor's Youth Council, newsletters for the youth, mentoring programs for children facing hardships in their life, and youth sports activities where I can volunteer to be a junior coach and help with the funds for snacks and equipment provided for the children.
Female, 12

Community service projects.
Male, 16

At University of Southern Mississippi, as part of the Gifted Studies program, they have a leadership program for a week in the summer each year. I went to that program one time. I learned so much there, and I plan to go to it again sometime.
Female, 14

Helping others in need.
Male, 13

Actions

Think About It

★ Do you have the same opportunities as those mentioned above? If not, how are they different?

★ What opportunities are there for being a leader in your community?

Write About It

★ Write a letter to the editor of your local newspaper outlining the reasons why more youth leadership opportunities should be provided in your community. Be sure to be positive and suggest ways this might happen.

★ Brainstorm a list of elected leadership positions for youth in the community and ways young people can be leaders in the community without being elected.

Do It

* If you need more information about the possibility of leadership opportunities for students in your community, ask your school counselor or contact the office of your mayor or Chamber of Commerce.

* Complete the following statement: I want to be a leader in my community because . . .

* Conduct a poll of your friends in other communities to determine the opportunities for being a leader. Make a composite list of the potential leadership opportunities in your community and compare and contrast it to the list you have received from other communities. How are they alike? How are they different? Are there opportunities for leadership in other communities that could be used in your own community?

* Contact three influential community leaders and tell them about the need for more leadership opportunities for youth. Ask for their help in taking action toward this goal.

* Contact community leaders in art, politics, education, business, and industry. Develop interview questions for them that focus on areas such as who or what influenced them to be leaders, what advice they would give to young leaders, and how they see leadership changing for the future. Use this information to develop an audio- or videotape, a booklet, or some other product that could be given to students in the community.

* For history buffs, trace the early leaders in your community and develop, in print form, a historical overview of the early influences of community leaders as well as how community leadership has changed over time. Investigate the process for getting this printed

and placed in your town's Chamber of Commerce office.

★ Make a collage of the way early leaders influenced major developments in your community.

★ Develop a list of community leaders who would like to be mentors to young leaders and organize a mentor experience for students of your age.

★ Develop a list of part-time jobs in your community that have opportunities for leadership and share it with others.

What Opportunities Do You Have for Being a Leader in Your Religious Organization?

Our survey said that students view their religious organization as providing a wide range of opportunities for being a leader. They included direct contact with those of their own ages, to serving on committees and boards with adults. Sponsored events within and outside the religious organization also offered opportunities for leadership.

Ideas

I help lead in children's choir. I participate in Bible drill.
I have achieved the highest level in our memory verse
program. I help organize community service projects.
Female, 9

Mission trips and weekend events (like Turning Point).
Female, 17

Helping out wherever it is needed.
Male, 16

Girl Scouts, Girls' Auxiliary, dance ministry, mime ministry,
drill team, and our church step team.
Female, 13

My opportunities for leadership in my community carry over
to my opportunities in leading in my church, providing people
in need with clean clothes and clean shelters, as well as
guiding them toward professional help.
Female, 13

In my church I lead and direct praise dances and give
youth leadership speeches.
Female, 12

I have opportunities to participate in programs and help the
elders. I have the opportunity to share my beliefs and tell
how they have helped me.
Female, 16

I can help on clean-up day. I can convince people to give their life over to God.
Male, 14

CYO—Christian Youth Organization.
Male, 16

Praying with others, becoming friends with new people.
Male, 16

The opportunities I have for being a leader in my church are associations such as: Youth in Praise Willing Workers (Y.P.W.W.), where youth members get a chance to have a voice of reason in portions of the Sunday services. I am also on the decorating committee where I show my creativity with décor for occasions, and I am a Sunday school assistant where my job is to help others understand biblical terminology.
Female, 12

Actions

Think About It

★ What leadership opportunities in your religious organization appeal to you?

★ Complete the following statement: I want to be a leader in my religious organization because . . .

★ Think of other opportunities that could be started in your religious organization.

Talk About It

★ Talk with the head of your religious organization to get his or her ideas on leadership activities in which you can be involved.

Write About It

★ Write an article for your religious organization's bulletin or newsletter about the need for more leadership activities for students.

Do It

★ Call your friends who attend other religious organizations. Make a list of leadership opportunities that are available for young persons in other religious organizations.

★ Brainstorm a list of leadership activities you would like available in your religious organization. Circle the one you think is the most important. Write a plan for getting this activity started.

★ Compare and contrast the list you made above to leadership opportunities in your religious organization. How are they alike? How are they different? Are there opportunities for leadership in other religious institutions that could be used in your religious organization? Brainstorm a list of elected and nonelected positions of leadership for young persons in your religious organization.

★ Design activities for younger students to encourage them to become leaders in their religious organization.

Training for Leadership

> What Opportunities Do You Have for Training in Leadership Concepts and Skills in Your School (e.g., Special Classes, Afterschool Programs, Workshops)?

Our survey found that students had several sources of training for leadership within their schools. The most typical examples were Student Council, special clubs, and programs for high-ability and gifted students. Summer programs focused on leadership training were available to a few students.

Some students perceived training as being unavailable or limited in their schools.

Ideas

Opportunities I have for training in leadership concepts are through team building and a communication course of instruction where students who are enthusiastic about running for positions in the Student Council learn to campaign and cooperate with the student body.
Female, 12

I am sure they are available but I am fairly new to this school, so I am not really sure.
Female, 17

Through the Key Club.
Male, 16

We have the Boys and Girls Club, which is an afterschool program. The family YMCA also has afterschool programs. The gifted education classes, which are in school, are another opportunity.
Female, 13

Currently, I am in the Florida state gifted program for junior high students, I am a member of the National Junior Honor Society, and I also attended The University of North Florida's Math, Science, and Engineering Camp for gifted students. I got nominated and accepted to attend the National Young Leaders' State Conference.
Female, 13

We have very few opportunities within my school; however, I am a member of the JROTC, Student Council, and Peer Council, which help us become better leaders.

Female, 16

I learn a great deal about leadership in Horizons, a program for gifted students.

Female, 9

When people at school come to me with their problems I can try to lead them on the right trail.

Male, 14

Opportunities to join school clubs.

Male, 13

My opportunities for training in leadership concepts and skills in school are for the Student Council and technology training.

Female, 12

Actions

Think About It

★ Does your school have more or fewer opportunities than the ones mentioned above? What other opportunities would you like to have available in your school?

★ In which opportunities would you like to participate?

Write About It

★ Write a short skit about teachers assisting students in developing their leadership skills.

★ Compile a directory of opportunities for leadership development in your school. Publish the results in your school newspaper and/or on the school Web site.

Do It

★ Present a brief skit at a faculty meeting or another appropriate group meeting of educators. Use humor as much as possible while expressing your important message about the need for more leadership training in the classroom.

★ Contact your principal, teacher, or guidance counselor and tell him or her about the kind of leadership development you would like to have in your school and offer to help plan the training.

★ Locate adult leaders who would be willing to devote time to training students in leadership concepts and skills. Set up a school resource file with these leaders' contact information.

★ Organize an afterschool leadership club in which you may read about and discuss famous leaders as well as leadership concepts and skills. Use the Leadership Books for Youth reading list found in the back of this book for suggestions (see page 197).

> What Opportunities Do You Have for Training in Leadership Concepts and Skills in Your Community (e.g., Workshops, Seminars)?

Our survey found that students in some communities have a variety of opportunities for leadership training available to them. Others appear to have created their own opportunities, and a few stated that there were none. Opportunities focused on those associated with clubs for students, participation with adults, and special situations that community leaders have established for youth.

Ideas

Helping with recreation activities.
Female, 13

My training in leadership concepts from my school carries over into the community. Members of the National Junior Honor Society have opportunities to shadow many people with leadership positions.
Female, 13

Just like in my school, opportunities for training in leadership are limited in my community. We only have a few programs that give us opportunities to go to seminars.

Female, 16

I can try to tutor in the afterschool program. This would help me by offering my help in a subject that they lack in.

Male, 14

The Leadership Studies Program at the University of Southern Mississippi.

Male, 16

An opportunity I have for training in leadership concepts in my community is attending weekly meetings at the local library where all youth help make useful decisions and inputs on changes for the community.

Female, 12

Not aware of any opportunities.

Male, 13

My opportunities for training in leadership concepts and skills in the community are Girl Scouts, Brownies, and the Mayor's Sports Club.

Female, 12

I have attended sports camps and Girl Scouts that emphasize leadership and citizenship.

Female, 9

Actions

Think About It

★ What generalizations or conclusions can you think of that are reflected in the responses on pages 69–70 about leadership training in the community?

★ What ideas can you and your friends come up with to motivate the adults in your community to help you get started in leadership development programs?

Do It

★ What kinds of youth leadership training programs exist in your community? Develop a resource file on these programs for others to use.

★ Identify influential leaders in your community. Get a group of other students interested in leadership development with adult leaders. Ask for their help in determining and implementing leadership training programs for youth. This may take a good bit of research on your part, but there are programs available!

★ Design a plan for leadership training for students younger than you. Get other youth leaders involved in helping you plan and implement your program. Be sure to get input from adult leaders before beginning this project as well as feedback by evaluating the project after it has been completed.

★ Conduct a survey of leadership training activities in your community and make a chart showing the results of the survey. Send it to your local paper and to your school newspaper or ask to be on a television or radio talk show to share these results. If there are not many existing leadership training programs, ask the television and radio audiences to offer ideas and assistance in developing such programs.

★ Conduct an analysis of existing leadership training programs. Who may attend the programs? What ages are the participants? What are the costs, if any? What are the goals and objectives of the program? Present this information to your local Chamber of Commerce or similar organization.

★ List the community leadership training programs in which you have been involved. State the positive and negative aspects of these programs. Develop a handbook of the ones you would recommend.

★ Contact local businesses in your community to determine the types of leadership training programs available for employees. Get their input on how these programs might be adapted for youth.

★ Develop a petition and get signatures from students and their parents who are interested in leadership training programs. Present it to the mayor or city manager and ask for a citywide youth leadership training program.

> ## What Opportunities Do You Have for Training in Leadership Concepts and Skills in Your Religious Organization (e.g., Workshops, Seminars)?

Our survey found that students felt that leadership training is generally available through religious organizations. Special seminars and workshops on leadership training are offered in many religious organizations and some students receive special leadership training in religious camps for youth.

Ideas

At our church there are no workshops but I lead by letting everyone know they can count on me for help.
> *Male, 16*

I have opportunities to help in the preschool class in Sunday school and Bible school. My church sponsors workshops that teach us how to be leaders.
> *Female, 9*

Help teach the different ministries.
> *Female, 13*

By attending youth seminars or Bible studies, I gain leadership concepts and skills, which help me tutor and educate younger members of my church.
Female, 13

Every Sunday is an opportunity for training in leadership. We also have programs that help us to grow as a person to be strong leaders.
Female, 16

I can lead the youth service. This would help me take charge when everything seems like it's falling apart.
Male, 14

I am on the greeting team and I serve on Sundays and greet and meet new people when they attend our church.
Male, 13

An opportunity I have for training in leadership concepts in my church is an assembly with the topics of how my church can improve our society's knowledge about Christ. We also train in communication skills with other people of different cultures and beliefs.
Female, 12

Actions

Think About It

★ Most religious organizations depend on the youth to help add enthusiasm and variety to their membership. How could you and other youth in your religious organization convince the adults that youth leadership training programs will develop and strengthen programs and will benefit your organization in many ways?

Do It

* Contact some of your friends and adult leaders in your religious organization. As a group, brainstorm ways for providing more training for leadership concepts and skills through various activities such as Sunday school, Hebrew school, choir, youth group, and study of religious writings.
* Plan a leadership lock-in for the youth of your religious organization. Organize activities that would get kids involved in skills of leadership such as speaking in front of a group, group problem solving, and planning youth projects. Discuss famous religious leaders. Select five famous religious leaders (past or present) and do research on their backgrounds. What leadership styles do/did they use? How do you feel they can be/could have been more effective as leaders? Write stories about these leaders for the younger children in your religious organization. Plan a time to present the stories to these children.
* If you could change society's attitude toward religion, what would you like to change, and how would you go about it?
* Survey members of your religious organization to determine those that could design a leadership training program for youth. Ask them to meet with you and develop a timeline for beginning the training activities.
* Select a religious leader (past or present) that you consider to be your role model. Write a letter or e-mail to

this person explaining why he or she is a role model for you. If the person is still living, send your letter or e-mail to him or her.

Influence and Encouragement From Others

Who or What Has Had the Most Influence on the Development of Your Leadership Abilities and Why?

Our survey found that family members, teachers and other school personnel, friends, and religious leaders were most often named as those influencing the leadership development of these youth. Participation in programs and caring for pets and others have also influenced leadership abilities.

Ideas

My oldest sister, Tyler, is mentally handicapped and has a lot of medical problems. Although some would think of it as a burden, I feel that living and working with her has made me a better person and a stronger leader.

Female, 17

My grandpa has had the most influence. He came from nothing without a college education and now is the head of the safety office at the corps of engineers and will do anything and everything to help anyone.

Male, 16

My mother has had the most influence because she demonstrates leadership skills in all areas of her life.

Female, 9

My community has helped me the most because the atmosphere that's around me teaches me that I can become more than I already am.

Female, 13

My parents are active leaders in the community, school, and church. By always doing what is necessary and putting others' needs first no matter how stressful the situations are they taught me that, "You can move a mountain one shovel at a time."

Female, 13

My mother has influenced me most because she has allowed me to attend different camps every summer since I was 6 years old. She always encourages me to do my very best everyday.

Female, 16

The most influence on the development of my leadership abilities has been my former gifted teacher, Ms. Rondon. She showed me the keys to being a leader and encouraged me to step forward and apply the qualities of leadership in my life.

Female, 12

My mother. She leads me by example. If she told me not to do something, usually she didn't do it either. She is intelligent, loving, and compassionate.

Male, 14

My basketball coaches.

Male, 16

My mom and the leadership program I went to. My mom because she gives great tips and talks to me about leadership a lot. I have a good bit of information from her. The leadership program really introduced me to what leadership is. From that, I know what a leader is, what a leader does, and so much more.

Female, 14

I have attended the leadership program at the [Frances A.] Karnes Center for Gifted Studies for 2 years. I use the skills I learned at the leadership program at school and at church. My youth pastor has also influenced my leadership skills.

Male, 13

The Frances A. Karnes Center for Gifted Studies has had the most influence on the development of my leadership abilities because it was organized with courses and instructors who had the ability to educate and mold me in a way that was simple for me to understand. The Center for Gifted Studies enhanced my knowledge of a realistic leader.

Female, 12

Actions

Think About It

★ Who has most influenced your leadership abilities?

★ What book or situation has had the most influence on your leadership abilities?

★ Select a leader from the past and think about his or her possible influence on you if you had lived during that period of time. Does he or she influence you now? How?

★ What person or persons have discouraged you from developing as a leader? How have they been obstacles to your leadership development?

Read About It

★ Read a biography or an autobiography of a leader and determine who influenced his or her leadership abilities.

Do It

★ Visit the persons in your community who have most influenced your leadership ability. Tell them why they are a role model for you and thank them for being an important part of your growth as a leader. Be sure to share the specific things they have done or said that have helped you.

How Can Parents Best Encourage Leadership Concepts and Skills in Their Children?

Our survey found that many suggestions were given as to how parents can best encourage leadership. Some of the suggestions were giving students responsibility in the home, allowing decision making on the part of students, listening to their ideas, and encouraging them to be leaders and to participate in school, community, and religious events. Students also stated that parents should praise them when they accomplish their goals. They wanted parents to provide leadership training activities for them outside of the home by allowing the students to attend training programs and seminars.

Ideas

Support both emotionally (and financially if needed); being there as "sounding board" to help problem solve.
Female, 17

Parents can allow them to take on responsibilities at home and within the community that compel them to be leaders.
Female, 9

By example. At work and at home they can know that teamwork is the best way to success and knowledge.
Male, 16

By pushing me to do my best and by bringing hope to the present and future.
Female, 13

Parents can best encourage leadership concepts and skills in their children by merely elucidating the facts of life and expressing leadership skills in their everyday lifestyles.
Female, 12

By giving children the opportunity and freedom to explore and ask questions and let them believe they can do and be anything they want to.
Female, 13

When situations come up in your child's life, listen. Don't just tell them, "Do it because I said so." If you do, your child won't know why he is doing it. This could lead to wrong choices made in the long run.
Male, 14

Parents can best encourage leadership concepts and skills in their children by giving them more responsibilities.
Female, 12

Parents should tell their children to be who they are. Leadership occurs naturally and should not be forced.

Male, 16

The best parents can do is just inform their children about leadership when they are ready. After that, they should observe their child and when they see [him or her] being a leader, they should bring it to the child's attention. Also, encourage [the child] to serve as a leader in [his or her] community or school.

Female, 14

By sending children to leadership development programs and by encouraging them to help others.

Male, 13

Actions

Think About It

★ What are your parents doing to encourage you to be a leader?

★ What else would you like them to do?

Do It

★ Talk with your parents about leadership and leaders. Do they know people in the community you could talk to about being a leader? Think of questions that you would like to ask these leaders. Contact the person(s) and make an appointment.

★ Developing responsibility is an important part of leadership. What responsibilities do you have in your family? Which ones do you want in the future to help you become more of a leader? Talk to your parents about possibly taking on new responsibilities and when you will begin.

★ Make a list of how your parents have influenced your leadership ability (positively or negatively) and share the list with them.

★ Brainstorm the ways you think you will help your own child become a leader. Write a letter to the child you hope to have and tell him or her about this.

★ Talk with your parents about allowing you to plan some of the following activities: a meal, a party, a family vacation, a shopping trip, or a family visit to a local nursing home. Other fun family activities you may want to plan are collecting toys and books for children in the hospital and organizing magazine collections for nursing homes. Use your imagination and your local resources!

★ After researching the home lives of great leaders, write some important ways parents influenced these great leaders and share these ideas with your own parents.

★ Get a group of your friends together. Design short skits that portray parents in opposite ways: situations in which parents do not encourage their children to be leaders and situations in which parents do encourage their children to be leaders. Present your skits to various groups of students and parents. You might share the skit with your school's Parent Teacher Association.

★ Get several friends together and prepare brief written statements describing why you think it's important for you to gain leadership concepts and skills. Arrange a meeting at your home or school for parents. Present your ideas and discuss the positive aspects of leadership for students.

How Can Teachers Best Encourage Leadership Concepts and Skills in Their Students?

Our survey found that students gave many suggestions on how teachers could best encourage leadership concepts and skills. Teachers should create environments in their classrooms that allow students to take more responsibility and build their self-confidence. Through discussions, students want to develop their thinking and creativity skills and become better speakers. Teachers should encourage students to be leaders and indicate the positive aspects of leadership. Students also said they would like information on school and club elections and opportunities to attend programs and seminars on leadership.

Ideas

Understanding the time that leadership requires and the encouragement. Also making opportunities available and letting us know what's out there.
Female, 17

Teachers can best encourage leadership concepts and skills in their students by letting them lead in discussion and group projects.
Female, 12

Teachers can best encourage leadership skills by teaching students how to do it and also show by example. They can show what they do in the community.
Male, 16

By taking the time to work with the students and by communicating leadership skills.
Female, 13

By allowing students to express their own opinions and enforcing individual as well as group activities. Also by giving them the opportunity to speak their voices and teaching them to agree to disagree.
Female, 13

The teacher should be a good leader. [Teachers] should encourage all students to do their very best everyday.
Female, 16

By example. Some students look up to teachers. If they see [teachers] doing something wrong, they might think it's okay.
Male, 14

Teachers can best encourage leadership concepts and skills in their students by assisting them with creative

 Leadership for Students

critiques and how to manage simple everyday conflicts or situations that can be avoided.

Female, 12

Encourage students to be who they are.

Male, 16

They can point it out to the class when they see a student being a leader. Then explain what to be a leader is and so on.

Female, 14

Teachers can provide group project opportunities that encourage students to take on leadership roles.

Female, 9

Teachers can encourage students to try hard in school and give them opportunities to help others.

Male, 13

Actions

Think About It

★ Think of all of the ways you could be a leader in your classroom and discuss these with your teacher. Ask him or her to help you develop more responsibilities.

Write About It

★ Write an editorial for your school newspaper on how teachers can and should promote leadership skills for youth. You may want to post it on the school Web site as well. Be sure to get permission first!

★ Compose a song or rap about teachers and leadership in the classroom.

Do It

★ Talk to your teacher, guidance counselor, or principal about the ways to demonstrate leadership in your school through clubs and groups. Make a list and decide which one you would like to join.

★ Think of a teacher who allows students to have some responsibilities within the class. Seek his or her assistance in designing a plan of action for getting other teachers in your school to help students become more responsible leaders.

★ Hold an election of the teachers in your grade. Have the students select the teacher who best encourages leadership development.

★ Make a list of the ways your teachers encourage leadership. Conduct an electronic survey with other young people about how their teachers encourage leadership. You could send one question, "How do your teachers encourage leadership?" out through Twitter or conduct a full survey. Your principal may be able to direct you to other county or state school e-mail addresses or you may use your state's department of education Web site to get those school e-mail addresses. It is best to go through your principal for help with this project. Compile your results and post them on your school Web site. Be sure to get permission first!

★ Design a poster, comic strip, or some other visual representation of the positive things that teachers do to promote leadership growth, as well as the negative things that teachers do that prevents leadership growth. Be sure not to use teachers' names! Share these with the faculty of your school.

★ Give a monthly award to the teacher who best promotes leadership in the classroom. You might design a cool certificate on your computer to give him or her or get local restaurants to donate a free meal or dessert. You also could designate a "Teacher Leaders Hall of Fame" bulletin board in the hall near the school office to post the photographs and awards of the teachers being recognized.

Great Leaders

> Who Do You Consider to Be One of the Greatest Leaders of All Time (Past and Present)? Why?

Our survey found that the names of political and government leaders were commonly offered as the greatest leaders, past and present, by the students. There were a few females viewed as being leaders. The majority of the leaders were of the past and not of the present. Interestingly, one girl perceived her parents to be the greatest leaders.

Ideas

I consider Barack Obama to be one of the greatest leaders of all times. He draws my attention by the confident way he carries himself, addresses his audience, and the context of his speeches. He is a living reminder of what I learned about Dr. Martin Luther King, Jr. in my history class and family discussions.

Female, 12

My mentally handicapped sister. Although she doesn't lead in the "normal" sense, she inspires others and makes them a better person. Personally, I believe that this is what makes a true leader.

Female, 17

Brett Favre because he came from a small town and took his college team to success. He also took his NFL team to success and still is the greatest quarterback and team leader of all time.

Male, 16

Martin Luther King, Sr. because he wanted what was best for the world and wanted to live the life of a fellow Christian. My mother led us to grow up and become successful; someone better than she was.

Female, 13

Cleopatra, the sixth pharaoh of Egypt. She was the first female leader of a highly developed and civilized society.

Female, 13

Past—Martin Luther King because so many people listened, followed, and respected him. He showed love for all people. Present—Billy Graham because he always speaks a message of hope.

Female, 16

Martin Luther King, Jr. He wasn't scared to try to change the world. He wasn't afraid of risk and because of that he made the world a better place.

Male, 14

I consider Ruth Rondon, my gifted studies teacher, to be one of the greatest leaders of all times because Ms. Rondon has the experience of a strong, Black woman who has survived the harsh world. Ms. Rondon has been through life's cruel struggles and has lived to see the day to provide the facts for others, so that they won't have to figure out life the hard way.

Female, 12

Past—Alexander the Great. I think conquering the known world in one's lifetime has its merits. Present—Gandhi because he led millions without using force.

Male, 16

I consider Martin Luther King, Jr. to be one of the greatest leaders. He is a man who possessed many great leadership qualities and influenced many. Many people followed him, and after he died there were many people who took over to continue what he started. That shows that he was a great leader because so many people followed him.

Female, 14

Jesus Christ; Martin Luther King, Jr.

Male, 13

I consider Jesus to be one of the greatest leaders of all times because He led through example and used positive persuasion to show people the way.

Female, 9

Actions

Think About It

★ Who do you consider to be one of the greatest leaders of all times and why?

★ What generalizations or big, connecting ideas could you make from the students' responses above?

★ How does your own response compare to the students' responses above?

★ Think of leaders who changed our lives but may not be known to many people.

★ It often has been said that a civilization can be described by a study of its moral and religious leaders. Do you agree or disagree? Can you think of specific examples?

Write About It

★ Write a scenario about fictional leaders of the future based on a futuristic problem and get it published in the school or local newspaper.

★ Research a great leader and write a speech to nominate the person for the "Leaders' Hall of Fame."

★ Create a fictional leader of the future (25 years from now) and write a story about how this leader's life and leadership present different challenges and require different skills than leaders of today.

★ Create riddles or puzzles about great leaders. Put them in a book for your friends.

★ Write an essay entitled, "The Best Leader I've Ever Known." Ask your principal to let you read it at the next school program. Ask your principal, English teacher, or mayor to sponsor a schoolwide essay contest on the same or a similar topic.

Do It

★ Create a scrapbook, diorama, mobile, or some other creative product to represent the life of a great leader.

★ Research great leaders to determine how their families fostered leadership ability. Share these ideas with your parents.

★ Research leaders and categorize them according to their leadership style (e.g., democratic, autocratic, *laissez faire*).

★ Research how great leaders build a power base and relate this to your own leadership goals.

★ Research a leader and identify why the person is considered a great leader, then develop a booklet on the person for younger students.

★ Research a leader of the past and predict how the person would lead on a current issue. For example, how would Abraham Lincoln solve apartheid in South Africa? How would Michelangelo help society become more art literate? How might Gandhi solve the conflicts in Iran or North Korea?

★ Research and compare and contrast the similarities and differences between leaders who had (or have) a negative influence on society with those who had (or have) a positive influence. Discuss this with your friends or your leadership groups at school.

★ Make a scrapbook of great leaders by collecting photographs and biographical information on leaders from the past and the present.

★ Have a "Great Leaders Party" at your home or in school. Everyone should come dressed as a great leader but should not reveal who he or she is. As you talk with each other at the party, you may ask questions that require a "yes" or "no" response in order to guess the identity of each person.

★ Using books, journals, and online resources to gather information about great leaders of the past and present, complete the Leadership Matrix on page 169. Be sure to include female and male leaders, as well as those from different ethnic and religious backgrounds.

Advice to
Others

> What Is the Best Advice You Could Give to Someone Who Wants to Become a Leader?

Our survey indicated that the responses show great depth and insight. Many students suggested training in leadership such as attending workshops, seminars, and classes. Others recommended reading books about leadership and researching past leaders, observing and following role models, and becoming involved in extracurricular activities.

Some students advised those who want to become leaders to work on weaknesses and build strengths and listen to and try to understand themselves. A few students cautioned potential leaders against being too pushy or obnoxious. They also warned others not to be conceited in leadership positions and not to lose sight of what it feels like to be a follower.

Ideas

Just do it! Don't wait for someone else.
Female, 17

The best advice I could give to someone who wants to become a leader is to be confident in yourself, have faith in your abilities, stay focused, and forever do your best.
Female, 12

First you need to learn your skills and then learn your teammates. Every person is different and you have to learn [that] you have to deal with each person in a different manner. And last but not least learn the ups and downs about your own personality.
Male, 16

Always stay true to yourself.
Female, 13

Go for it! Never give up, and never be afraid to ask for help.
Female, 13

The best advice I could give to someone who wants to become a leader is to be prepared and do not expect anything to be given to you—you must be willing to fight for it.
Female, 12

Apply yourself, learn a lot, love all people, and be open-minded. Believe in yourself and take a stand. My mother always says to do the right thing.
   Female, 16

Go for it. Don't let somebody tell you what you can and can not do. It is your life to live; you only get one. Shoot for the moon and if you miss you will be among the stars.
   Male, 14

I believe that one should not look to be a leader, but if one possesses qualities of leadership, people will follow.
   Male, 16

Just put your best foot forward and try to use every talent you have. You want to put your best foot forward because you want to give it your all. By that I mean if you run for president of a club and you don't win, don't give up, keep trying and work on your leadership skills, so when you get the chance you will be the best. Every leader has a talent, and they should try to use that talent to help them lead.
   Female, 14

Attend a leadership program, find ways to help others, and be an honest and truthful person.
   Male, 13

I would tell them to not be afraid to express their thoughts and opinions. I would tell them to be assertive and speak up but to always respect the ideas and opinions of others.

Female, 9

Actions

Think About It

★ Select the statements listed above that best describe the advice you would give someone. What makes it the best advice?

★ Is there other advice that you would give a person wanting to be a leader?

★ Develop a motto or a mission statement that states the advice that you would give someone about being a leader.

★ What is the best advice that you can give yourself on becoming a leader?

★ Many quotes on leadership have been provided for you in this book. Which ones are the most representative of advice you think is best?

★ What advice do you think our current president would give for becoming a leader?

Do It

★ Close your eyes and picture yourself as a leader in 6 months or a year. Keep your eyes closed and continue to think about your leadership position when you finish college. Make a list of the kinds of leadership positions that you would like to have in your community, school, or religious affiliation in the next 5 years.

* Survey other students in your school to get their ideas on the best advice for someone wanting to become a leader. Design a poster of this advice and display it in the hallway. Share it with younger students, too!

* Survey adult leaders in your school, community, or religious organization to get their ideas on the best advice for someone wanting to become a leader. Design a poster of this advice. Compare and contrast the students' advice to the adults' advice. How are they alike? How are they different?

* Choose five great leaders and develop a skit based on the advice that they would give on becoming a leader.

* Write, produce, and videotape a television commercial for leadership encouraging younger students to become leaders. Post the commercial on YouTube. Be creative with your message of the importance of leadership!

* Create a new game on how to become a leader. Think of all of the setbacks or obstacles that a leader may face. This may make your game more interesting!

Individual and Group Leadership Accomplishments

ART FOR SPECIAL HEARTS

EVER since Shelby was a little girl she has had a love for art. As a 17-year-old high school senior, it was her desire to share this passion with others who might not otherwise have a creative outlet. In 2008, she started Art for Special Hearts (ASH). This monthly program partners with The Arc, allowing special needs women to express themselves through arts and crafts.

Art always has been Shelby's passion and serves as her outlet for expression. She could not imagine a day without the ability to draw, paint, or create. Shelby started Art for Special Hearts to provide the opportunity for women with mental handicaps to experience this same joy from art. She wanted them to be included, not judged. She wanted them to be successful, not left out. Most importantly, she wanted the community to realize that these individuals are truly special, not just disabled.

Unlike most of her friends, Shelby knows firsthand what obstacles an individual with special needs faces. Her 21-year-old sister, Tyler, has a mental disability. Ty helped inspire the initial idea. Now ASH is a monthly program, reaching an average of 15 women, from the ages of 16 to 66.

Some might think that having a sibling with special needs would be a burden for Shelby. However, she has never known anything different. Although she prays for her older sister to be healed from her medical problems and for her pain to end, she cannot imagine her life without Ty. Shelby will tell you that living with an individual with a mental disability gives a person a new and different perspective on life. Seeing the world through Ty's eyes reminds her of the joy of new experiences, the excitement that simple things possess, and the gift of unconditional love. Ty's innocence is pure and untainted and she reminds all of us of what is really important. Her sister also has taught Shelby that most communities don't understand the obstacles of individuals with mental disabilities. The special needs population doesn't want to be "different" although they usually are isolated and left out of "normal" activities. People often are cruel and judgmental about things they don't understand.

Shelby created every aspect of Art for Special Hearts (even the name). With the help of a local art studio, she arranged the donation of an appropriate space where the women could work without limitations. No one cares if they are messy or loud or "different." Everyone is just excited that they are there and inspired by their smiles and their innocent, genuine joy. The end result is a tangible creation that each woman can display with pride and a great sense of accomplishment.

The most difficult part of this project was simply getting started. The vision was easy but the details were overwhelming at first for Shelby. Fortunately, she works at a local art studio and her employers are supportive of this endeavor. They not only donated the space for ASH but also helped with the first craft ideas and provided supplies. Other members of her community also generously donated items to help with the expenses.

Getting volunteers for the monthly Saturday activities was the easiest aspect. Several of Shelby's friends, both boys and girls, were quick to offer their help. After almost a year, she will tell you that she's not sure who enjoys the Saturdays more, the women or the volunteers!

Selecting the clients of The Arc's women's respite was a natural choice. Shelby had volunteered for other Arc programs because of her family involvement and her sister, Tyler, has been a member of this organization for the last 14 years. This connection made the partnership easy. The Arc staff members help by providing transportation for the women for each Saturday outing.

Most would assume that the most pronounced impact of this project was on each of the women who are mentally disabled. In truth, the benefits extend to everyone involved. The volunteers work one Saturday a month, donating their time and talents. What they receive is the opportunity to step out of their comfort zone, to learn from someone with different life experiences, and to receive true, unconditional love. The community, as a whole, learns acceptance of those who are different, realizing that everyone has creativity and a unique perspective. The women learn that they are valued. More importantly, they realize that they are special, not because they are different but because they make a positive difference to every life they touch.

Shelby has learned many things from this experience. She now realizes that the most precious gift you can offer someone is your time, your love, and your unconditional acceptance. These are the things that we often take for granted and things that can potentially change the world. Shelby's message is that we should all find our passions and share them with others.

A SPECIAL WISH FOR A SPECIAL BOY

O N a bright and sunny spring day in April, Madison, her sister Regan, and her brother Logan met a very special boy named Joey. Although he could not walk very well and communicated using his hands to make words, Joey had a sparkling smile and charming way about him. He would grab Madison by the hand to show her all of the flowers in his backyard. Joey even picked a beautiful yellow rose and placed it in her hair. He would summon Logan to ride in his green tractor with him. Then he would gesture with his hands for Regan to come and push him in the big wooden porch swing. Joey loved to swing, slide, and play like other 8-year-old boys, but he had never been to a real playground in his entire life. He had a rare disease that made him very sick all of the time and kept him from being able to go to school or play with large groups of children. Joey's one wish was to have a giant playground in his backyard where he could play like a regular little boy.

Madison went home that day feeling very sad for Joey. He was so loving and full of life, but he was unable to experience the normal adventures of childhood. Madison and Regan tried for many days to come up with a plan to help Joey, but it was through Logan that they discovered a brilliant idea by accident. Logan said that they should ask the tooth fairy to grant Joey a wish. At first, Madison dismissed this idea as silly, but then her face lit up with excitement. She had recently helped her mother donate money to the Make-A-Wish Foundation.

Madison eagerly began to research everything she could find about the Make-A-Wish Foundation. She discovered that this foundation grants wishes to children like Joey with terminal and chronic diseases. Madison immediately shared her plan with Regan and Logan. They would help to get Joey's wish for his own playground granted.

Madison's and Joey's mothers worked together to complete the application process. Because she is a physical therapist, Madison's mother was asked to help design the playground to meet Joey's needs. Madison's mother also recruited Madison, Regan, and Logan to help design the playground because they were so determined to help Joey.

Madison came up with the idea for a hammock swing so that Joey could look at the sky when he swings. Regan suggested a tunnel slide so Joey would not fall out since his balance was not very good. Logan's idea was to design Joey a huge playhouse within the playground that resembled a pirate ship. He wanted Joey to have a real captain's wheel, binoculars, and a periscope. Their ideas were given to Rainbow Play Systems, Inc., a company that builds playgrounds.

The day finally arrived for Joey's playground to be completed in his backyard. Everyone was invited to a big party to celebrate Joey's wish coming true. Madison pushed Joey in the big hammock swing; Regan went down the yellow tunnel slide with him; and Logan played Pirates of the Caribbean with Joey on the pirate ship playground. Joey was happier than he had been in his entire life. For the first time ever, he was able to play on a real playground. It was a dream come true for Joey.

Madison lay in her bed that night thinking of everything that had led up to his spectacular day. She realized that although she had not received a gift today, she felt that she had been given the greatest gift of all. She finally understood the saying, "It is better to give than to receive" because today was not only the best day of Joey's life but the best day of Madison's life as well. She discovered that true happiness comes in giving to someone like Joey, and the returns that she felt from this gift were more glorious than any gift that she had ever been given.

Madison, Regan, and Logan tell all of their friends about their experience helping to grant Joey's wish. They want their friends to know the joy of helping others and the importance of being a leader and advocate for children with special needs. They have shared with their friends how to use perseverance, determination, and creativity to help make a little boy's wish come true.

THE 13TH OAK RACE

A FEW weeks before October 20, 1979, Armenia, an eighth grader at Shelby Oaks Middle School, experienced the tragic loss of her mother to cancer. Armenia remained confused for a long period of time. She didn't understand why her mother had to be taken away from this earth. Armenia made good grades, she was an obedient child, and loved her mother dearly. But as the days went by, she realized that in order to get somewhere, you have to go through something. She became certain that she wanted to help individuals to cope with cancer and assist other families with grief as they lost their lost loved ones to cancer.

For months, she was determined to increase her community's awareness of the death rate for cancer. She knew she had the potential and motivation to generate a sensational event to help bring about and sustain peoples' interest in helping to cure cancer. Along with obesity, cancer had killed a large amount of her community's population in Connecticut. With this in mind, she realized how she could take a small step that could help make a big change. Armenia created a title for her project to help fight cancer: The 13th Oak Race. According to Armenia, the title included the number 13 to represent the age she was when she began to understand the struggles of life, the word oak was included for the relationship of a tree that stands tall and is difficult to bring down, and race stood for the competition between a person and a fatal disease. Now all she had to do was get the money and support to complete her mission.

Armenia began to write a letter to the mayor to request help with the funds:

Dear Mayor Thomas,

    I am writing this letter to make inquiries for assistance with finances for an advantageous experience. My mother recently passed from cancer and I would like to organize a race for people interested in helping raise funds for cancer survivors and organizations in affiliation with cancer. I am eager to amplify our society's attention to this illness and show how people can influence and support others. This is a task that I am determined to fulfill.

Sincerely,

Armenia

A few weeks later, Armenia received a letter directly from the mayor. Her proposal was approved! She had now completed her first successful step. Afterward, Armenia started advertising The 13th Oak Race. Hoping that this was an invitation that people could not refuse, she was stunned by the motivation of people to get involved. Thousands of people from around different areas of Connecticut wanted to take part in this beneficial opportunity.

The 13th Oak Race has been celebrating cancer survivors since 1980. With this program, organizations walk or run a 10k, 5k, or 1-mile course. While supporting cancer survivors, they are also helping raise funds for cancer research. People donate money to other affiliations assisting cancer research and the families of those who have fought and died from cancer.

On your mark, get set, go! It is time to put on your comfortable shoes and brace yourself for the inspirational race of a lifetime. Now is the time to put your best foot forward and help raise money for your community. Armenia prevailed in her decision to help fight cancer with strength of mind, self-encouragement, and leadership.

WHAT GOES AROUND COMES AROUND!

VICTORIA is a student like you. At an early age Victoria knew that she wanted to help others in life so she took on a small project at her church that not only made a difference to others' lives but soon impacted her own.

Every year, Victoria and her family participated actively with their church in Burglengenfeld, Germany, in the Back

Packs for Orphans Drive. Members of the church would fill backpacks with necessary school supplies for orphans in Hungary. It was one of the member's duties to add something personal to each bag so that the child receiving it would feel special; sometimes it was a stuffed animal, a short note, a hairpin, a pack of cards, or new underwear. In 2000, Victoria was finally old enough to participate in the program. That year she was in charge of writing short notes of encouragement that she would then add to each bag. Carefully she would check the list to find out if the bag was for a boy or girl as well as the age of the child, and then she would write a note accordingly. This act took quite a bit of time considering that the church had taken on an orphanage that housed more than 150 school-age children. However, Victoria was determined to make sure all of the orphans received a kind and encouraging personal note. Sometimes she would even try to imagine how that child would react to what she had written, hoping it would bring a smile to the receiver's face.

Victoria participated in this program for 3 school years until her father was transferred to a new job in Mississippi. Soon that small task of writing those notes was forgotten.

In 2005, Victoria ended up becoming one of so many Gulf Coast residents who lost their homes and belongings to Hurricane Katrina. After 3 long weeks of living in her parents' car with only the clothes on her back, she and her family ended up at a Red Cross shelter in Florida.

While her parents were busy filing paperwork and handling insurance claims at that shelter, one of the Red Cross workers waved her over to follow her into a small, closet-like room. Shyly, she and her two brothers followed that lady into a closet filled with backpacks. Victoria and her brothers each picked up one and than sat quietly on the cot and eagerly inspected the backpack's contents. You should have seen the look on Victoria's face when she pulled out a small teddy bear with a note attached—a note that looked so much like one of the many she had written herself. But this time, she was the receiver of it. The note, carefully handwritten, stated: "Even though it doesn't seem like it right now, each day will get a little better and bring you closer to a happier time. Hopefully, the things in this bag will bring you a little happiness. We hope you are safe and well and we are thinking of you."

At this moment Victoria realized that life can change from one second to the next. Reading those words made Victoria remember how she used to imagine the looks on the children's face when they would read her notes. What goes around comes around—once she was the sender of notes like this, but now she was the receiver.

Shortly after she received that backpack and that note, Victoria started school in a new city in Florida.

In her first year at this school, she was elected for Student Council president, and her first mission was a drive for Dignity U Wear. Knowing how much little things can mean for a person, Victoria convinced her council team to join her. Victoria and the Student Council sent out letters to parents, teachers, local businesses, and churches, asking people to donate new underwear for their cause. With a team effort they gathered 6,000 pairs of underwear for children and adults.

Victoria had learned from her life experience that what goes around will come around, and she is convinced that what ever you do will come back to you. Victoria's advice to young people is to take the initiative in community projects and help out in any way possible. And, therefore, it's her mission to help others in every possible way.

ONE CUP AT A TIME!

JACKIE had always loved lemons: She loved to practice juggling lemons; she loved to scoop them out of her mother's iced tea and dip them in sugar; and she loved to slice them and squeeze their juice into a glass, add just the right amount of sugar and water, and make home-made lemonade. Nothing tasted better on a hot Southern summer day! But it wasn't until June 2008 when Jackie asked her Mom if she could have a lemonade stand that she truly realized the full potential of lemons. Her mom, Trish, agreed but only on the condition that the proceeds of her stand would benefit a good cause. Jackie was so excited and couldn't wait to get started but needed to decide what charity to select.

Jackie and her family moved to the south from New Jersey when she was 8 years old. Although it was hard to leave all of her family and friends in New Jersey, she quickly made friends in her new hometown. Jackie remembered seeing lemonade stands for pediatric cancer patients back in New Jersey and asked her Mom to help her research them. Her mom said they were called Alex's Lemonade Stands in honor of a cancer patient named Alex who came up with the idea of raising money for cancer research with her stand. Jackie researched online and found Alex's Web site (http://www. alexslemonade.org/home). It was full of inspiring stories of young cancer survivors and others who were fighting for their lives. After reading Alex story of her battle with cancer and realizing that this little girl, who was so sick, still wanted to help others, Jackie knew she could help, too. And when she read Alex's motto, "Fighting Childhood Cancer, One Cup at a Time," she knew she had found her cause! Jackie realized that the Annual Lemonade Days were coming up, during which thousands of lemonade stands across the country are set up to help raise money for childhood cancer, and no one had registered a stand in Mississippi. She knew she had to be that stand! She registered her stand for June 6, 2008, and set out to make it happen.

Where would she hold her stand? She needed a spot with lots of visibility, foot traffic, and, of course, a safe area for Jackie and her friends to set up their stand. Her new home-town in Mississippi was located in a pretty rural area so her house was not an option. The town did have a busy down-town area filled with shops, restaurants, offices, banks, a town hall, and a convention center. The sidewalk in front of the convention center made an ideal spot. But she needed per-mission from the Mayor and City Council to hold it on city property. Jackie and her Mom went to the Mayor's office to be put on the schedule for the upcoming meeting. She was nervous about speaking to the Mayor and the six council members but with a little guidance from her mom, she was able to tell them about Alex and how she wanted to represent Mississippi in the National Lemonade Days event. The Mayor and the council members were very supportive and even made the first donation!

A few days before the lemonade stand, Jackie and her friend Emma went downtown to hang up flyers. After they had finished hanging up the flyers, they went back to Emma's house where the local TV station interviewed Jackie about her lemonade stand. After the interview, Jackie and her mom went home to make posters for the lemonade stand.

The big day finally arrived! They loaded the car with all of their supplies and went to set up the lemonade stand. When Jackie and her mom reached the lemonade stand site, they noticed Emma and her mom were already there to help set up. After setting up the lemonade stand, one by one, Jackie's friends started coming with smiles on their faces. When everyone was there, some girls went to stand on nearby street corners to help market the lemonade stand while others stayed and ran the stand. A big group from the daycare center at a local church came by. Most of the kids carried coins in Ziploc bags to donate. They colored and drank lemonade and ate cookies. Throughout the day, more and more people dropped by to get lemonade. Sometimes people would hand donations out of their car windows to the workers. In addition, Jackie was interviewed again by a local TV station and was featured in a story on the front page of the local newspaper. At the end of the day, they had raised $2,000 for Alex's Lemonade Stand! Jackie and her friends were so proud!

The following year Jackie couldn't wait to do the lemonade stand again. This time she wasn't so nervous talking to City Council. She decided to give half of the money to a local camp for children with cancer called Camp Rising Sun and half to Alex's Lemonade Stand—two great charities with the same goal: helping children with cancer. She recruited even more friends to help. With the permission of her headmaster, she organized a workday in her school's gym where the students made posters and painted T-shirts. Afterwards, Jackie and her friends went to hang flyers at all of the downtown businesses. It was a lot of work but she knew it was worth it.

On the day of the lemonade stand, Jackie and her friends helped set up the stand, and like the previous year, some girls stood on street corners with posters and others stayed at the stand. Jackie was interviewed by the local TV station and had her picture in the local newspaper. Once again, Jackie and her friends raised more than $2,000, and this was split between the two charities. The girls learned that even 12-year-olds could make a difference "One Cup at a Time!"

Leadership
Action Journal

Chapter 1
Journal Entries

Defining Leadership

LEADERSHIP DEFINITIONS

Complete these definitions.

My definition of leadership is:

My friends' definitions of leadership are:

My definition of leadership for the 21st century is:

LEADERSHIP JOURNAL

BUMPER STICKER

Design a bumper sticker that represents your concept of leadership.

LEADERSHIP COMPARISONS

Complete these leadership comparisons. Be creative!

The color of leadership is

because

The smell of leadership is

because

The taste of leadership is

because

The touch of leadership is

because

The sound of leadership is

because

LEADERSHIP WEB

How is leadership connected to each of the parts of the web?

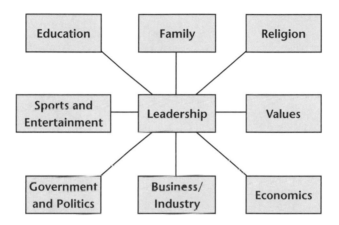

Write about all of the connections from the web on this page. For example, how is leadership seen in sports and entertainment? How does that differ from leadership in government and politics?

CHARACTERISTICS SELF-RATING

List the characteristics of leadership and rate yourself.
1 = I have this characteristics; 2 = I need to improve it; 3 = I
need to develop it

Characteristics	Self-Rating

LEADERSHIP JOURNAL

LEADERSHIP: NATURE OR NURTURE

Complete these statements with your own thoughts and what you can find in research about leadership development. Debate your friends and family about this!

Qualities/Skills of Leadership People Are Born With	Qualities/Skills of Leadership That People Must Learn

CHANGES IN LEADERSHIP OVER TIME

Research how leadership has been demonstrated throughout history. Make brief notes about how leaders worked with people in each historical situation. Then compare these notes to how leaders in today's society work. How are they the same? Different?

Tribal Leadership

Leadership in Royalty

Democratic Leadership

Cooperative or Shared Leadership

Leadership in Today's Society

LEADERSHIP JOURNAL

LEADERSHIP POSITIVES

Design a poster of famous leaders and include what each would say are the positive aspects of leadership.

LEADERSHIP NEGATIVES

Not all aspects of leadership are positive. List what you consider to be the negative aspects of leadership and how you can turn them into positives.

Negatives ———————————————————▶ Positives

Chapter 2
Journal Entries

Assessing Yourself as a Leader

WHAT KIND OF
LEADER ARE YOU?

LEADERSHIP JOURNAL

Using these questions as a guide, determine your natural style of leadership.

Style I: Controlling (Telling)

★ Do you do most of the planning and decision making?

★ Do you expect people to do what they are told and to bring problems to you?

★ Do you usually communicate the goals, methods, and timetables to your followers?

★ Do you often check closely behind people to see what progress is being made?

Style II: Consulting (Selling)

★ Do you set goals after talking with your group members and considering their ideas?

★ Do you listen to your group members and keep them well-informed?

★ Do you interact with them often?

★ Do you work hard to understand people's problems and help them solve them?

★ Do you support members of your group and give them positive feedback?

★ Do you treat people with respect as individuals?

★ Do you let people know when their performance is not what it should be and the consequences of poor performance?

Style III: Coaching (Participating)

★ Do you communicate expectations, goals, and boundaries?

★ Do you encourage your group members to structure their own work within the guidelines?

* Do you encourage people to solve their own problems and to seek help when needed?
* Do your group members feel comfortable talking with you in an open and honest way?
* Do you provide a lot of deserved, genuine, specific, positive, and negative feedback on performance?

Style IV: Delegating (Low-Key Approach to Influencing Others)

* Do you provide a general definition of what needs to be done with some structure?
* Do you allow your group members to provide their own structure and definition within limits?
* Do you let people do their work on their own with very little follow up or feedback?
* Do make informal checks when asked for help by group members?
* Do you provide help, encouragement, or support in limited amounts or when group members ask for it?

From the list above, determine which style is most like you. Remember that an effective leader knows how and when to use each of these styles. For example, sometimes you may have a group that knows exactly what needs to be done and how to do it. With that group, you probably need to be more of a Style III or Style IV leader. On the other hand, if you are working with a group that is unfamiliar with the work that needs to be done, a group whose members do not get along very well, or a group that is not motivated to do what needs to be done, you need to exercise more of Style I or Style II. Hersey and Blanchard (1982) called this approach *situational leadership*.

LEADERSHIP JOURNAL

LEADERSHIP ANALYSIS

Think about one successful and one unsuccessful leadership experience you have had. Describe each fully by answering the following questions.

Where and when did it take place? Who initiated it?

Who was involved? What was your role? What were the results?

What motivated you to assume leadership? What risks, if any, did you take?

LEADERSHIP JOURNAL

LEADERSHIP ANALYSIS, CONTINUED

What were your initial feelings? What did you feel at the project's end?

How did you encourage cooperation? Keep up enthusiasm?

How did you lead by example? Communicate your values?

LEADERSHIP JOURNAL

LEADERSHIP ANALYSIS, CONTINUED

Is there something different you could have done to be more effective in each case?

What was the single most important factor in your success and lack of success as a leader in these projects?

What can you learn from these experiences or use to improve your performance as a leader?

GROWING IN LEADERSHIP

John Maxwell (2002) said that successful leaders are learners and the learning process is ongoing, requiring self-discipline and perseverance. He says that leadership development happens in the following four phases.

Phase I: I Don't Know What I Don't Know

Some people don't understand the value of leadership and they believe that leadership is only for a chosen few. They have no idea what they are passing up by not learning to lead. They don't realize that leadership is influence and in the course of each day, most people try to influence at least four other people. They don't know that leadership is a behavior, not a position. As long as a person doesn't know what he doesn't know, he doesn't grow.

Phase II: I Know What I Don't Know

At some point in life people may realize that they need to learn how to lead and that's when the growth process starts. Benjamin Disraeli said, "To be conscious that you are ignorant of the facts is a great step to knowledge." In this phase people start reading about leadership and observing leaders and gathering resources. With this book, you have started this process.

Phase III: I Grow and Know and It Starts to Show

Exciting things will start to happen when you recognize your lack of skill and begin the daily practice of self-assessment, individual growth, and growth in working with other people. It won't happen in a day but you will see your influence growing greater and your leadership effectiveness will develop over time.

LEADERSHIP JOURNAL

Phase IV: I Simply Go Because of What I Know

You can be an effective leader but you must be conscious of your actions and the actions of others. You also must continue to learn about leadership: attend programs and seminars, gather resources, study people, study yourself, and learn from every experience. Pretty soon, your ability to lead will become automatic.

Where are you in your leadership growth? Write about how you see yourself growing as a leader. Develop a plan for growth.

SAMPLE CAMPAIGN
SPEECH OUTLINE

Use the following as a guide to help you prepare an outline for a campaign speech.

I want to run for this office because:

My strengths are:

My goals for this office are:

You should vote for me because:

Set goals that are possible. Only promise what you can do. Remember to be creative in how you deliver your thoughts. Humor works well, but don't overdo it!

LEADERSHIP JOURNAL

MY LEADERSHIP ROLES IN SCHOOL, MY COMMUNITY, AND MY RELIGIOUS ORGANIZATION

Fill in the chart below and then complete the sentences.

Ways I Have Been a Leader in School	Ways I Have Been a Leader in the Community	Ways I Have Been a Leader in My Religious Organization

Circle the leadership roles you have enjoyed the most.

The reasons why I liked the roles I circled are:

The reasons why I didn't like the noncircled roles are:

Extracurricular activities in which I would like to be involved and strategies for doing so are:

PLAN FOR A "LEADER OF THE MONTH" PROGRAM

Write your answers to the following questions.

What is the purpose of the proposed program?

How will you promote it?

Who will you need to help you get started?

What qualifications will be required to be recognized as "Leader of the Month?"

How will the recipients be selected?

Leadership for Students, 2nd Edition • Copyright © Prufrock Press Inc. This page may be photocopied or reproduced with permission for individual use.

L E A D E R S H I P   J O U R N A L

PLAN FOR A "LEADER OF THE MONTH" PROGRAM, CONTINUED

How will the recipients be recognized?

What local businesses or groups will help support this program?

What are other ways you can promote and advertise the program?

What creative ways can you come up with for getting other young people excited about the program?

How might you develop a Web site about the program? Get your school's technology teacher to help you with this. Set up a place on the Web site for students to blog about their leadership experiences.

STRONG AREAS OF LEADERSHIP SKILL

Think about your strengths in the area of leadership and respond to the items below.

List your strengths in leadership skills.

Put those same strengths in order of strongest to weakest.

Select a leader you admire and list his or her strengths in the area of leadership.

How do they compare to your strengths?

LEADERSHIP METAPHORS

Complete the following metaphors.

A leader is like a _____ because:
(animal)

A leader is like a _____ because:
(inanimate object)

A leader is like a _____ because:
(plant)

A leader is like a _____ because:
(shape)

A leader is like a _____ because:
(force of nature)

LEADERSHIP JOURNAL

WEAK AREAS OF
LEADERSHIP SKILL

Think about your areas of weakness in leadership and brainstorm some ideas for improvement.

Weaknesses	Strategies for Improvement

Ask an adult who is close to you to discuss these ideas for improvement with you.

LEADERSHIP JOURNAL

Chapter 3
Journal Entries

Opportunities for Leadership

OPPORTUNITIES FOR LEADERSHIP IN THE SCHOOL

Complete the following statements.

I would like to have the following opportunities for leadership in my school:

I plan to develop more opportunities for leadership in my school by:

LEADERSHIP POSITIONS
IN MY SCHOOL

List all of the scholastic and sports leadership positions in your school. Circle the ones that are the most important to you.

Scholastic Positions	Sports Positions

Develop a plan to lead one or two of the above positions.

LEADERSHIP JOURNAL

LEADERSHIP POSITIONS IN MY SCHOOL, CONTINUED

List all of the elected and unelected positions in your school. Circle the ones that are most important to you.

Elected Positions of Leadership in the School	Ways That a Person Can Be a Leader in School Without Being Elected to Office

LEADERSHIP JOURNAL

OPPORTUNITIES FOR LEADERSHIP IN MY COMMUNITY

Complete the following statement.

I want to be a leader in my community because:

LEADERSHIP JOURNAL

OPPORTUNITIES FOR CHANGE IN MY COMMUNITY

Make a list of things that you would like to begin or change in your community.

Begin	Change

Make a plan to begin or change one of these areas.

COMMUNITY LEADERS AS MENTORS

Make a list of community leaders who may serve as mentors to you and other young leaders. Contact these potential mentors and ask for a time when they can meet with you and allow you to observe them in their leadership activities.

Mentor	Area of Interest
Name:	
Address:	
Phone:	
E-mail:	

Mentor	Area of Interest
Name:	
Address:	
Phone:	
E-mail:	

Mentor	Area of Interest
Name:	
Address:	
Phone:	
E-mail:	

Mentor	Area of Interest
Name:	
Address:	
Phone:	
E-mail:	

LEADERSHIP JOURNAL

151

OPPORTUNITIES FOR LEADERSHIP IN MY RELIGIOUS ORGANIZATION

Brainstorm the various leadership positions, elected and otherwise, that are available in your religious organization.

Elected Positions of Leadership for Young People in Your Religious Organization	Ways That a Young Person Can Be a Leader in a Religious Organization Without Being Elected

Make a list of leadership activities you would like available in your religious organization.

Circle the one you think is most important. Develop and carry out a plan for getting the activity started.

Chapter 4
Journal Entries

Training for Leadership

SCHOOL FILE OF RESOURCE PEOPLE FOR LEADERSHIP TRAINING

Develop a resource file of persons who have had special training in leadership. Contact them to talk with your student body or to help conduct a special leadership training session for students.

Person	Area of Leadership Training
Name: Address: Phone: E-mail:	
Person Name: Address: Phone: E-mail:	Area of Leadership Training
Person Name: Address: Phone: E-mail:	Area of Leadership Training
Person Name: Address: Phone: E-mail:	Area of Leadership Training

COMMUNITY FILE OF LEADERSHIP PROGRAMS FOR YOUTH

List opportunities you have for training in your community.

Program Name	Contact Information	Type of Program
	Name: E-mail:	
	Name: E-mail:	
	Name: E-mail:	
	Name: E-mail:	
	Name: E-mail:	
	Name: E-mail:	

LEADERSHIP JOURNAL

COMMUNITY LEADERSHIP TRAINING PROGRAMS THAT I HAVE ATTENDED

List the names of leadership training programs that you have attended and include both the positive and negative aspects of each.

Program	Positive Points	Negative Points

Develop a handbook of the programs that you would recommend for others.

Chapter 5
Journal Entries

Influence and Encouragement
From Others

PARENTAL INFLUENCES ON LEADERSHIP

Think about your responsibilities at home and complete the following.

My current responsibilities at home:

Responsibilities I would like to have at home:

Talk with your parents about these responsibilities and set up a plan for getting started.

LEADERSHIP JOURNAL

LEADERSHIP INFLUENCES

List people in each category. Contact the persons listed in Part I to thank them. Contact the persons listed in Part II to ask for their help.

I.

People Who Have Already Influenced Me to Be a Leader	How They Have Influenced My Leadership Abilities

II.

Persons Who Could Have an Influence on My Leadership Abilities in the Future	How They Could Be of Help to Me as I Develop Leadership Skills

ENCOURAGING YOUR FUTURE CHILDREN

Think about your future children and complete the following statements.

Dear Children:
My hopes for you as a leader are:

I will try to be a good leader and role model for you by:

It is important to me that you learn to make decisions because:

Other ways I plan to help you develop as a leader are:

If you feel comfortable with your responses, share these with your parents. It may help them learn other ways they can encourage you as a leader.

TEACHERS' INFLUENCE

Write your responses to these and other statements about leadership in an editorial. Get other responses from students of all races, genders, and socioeconomic levels. Share these with your principal and teachers.

Teachers can have a very positive influence on their students' leadership ability by:

Sometimes teachers discourage leadership in their students by:

Sometimes school elections are based on popularity rather than leadership. Teachers could help discourage this by:

Leadership is an important area to be developed in the youth of today because:

Leadership for Students, 2nd Edition • Copyright © Prufrock Press Inc. This page may be photocopied or reproduced with permission for individual use.

LEADERSHIP JOURNAL

Chapter 6
Journal Entries

Great Leaders

ANALYSIS OF GREAT LEADERS

There are many great leaders in your hometown and in your state. Brainstorm a list of people in your area that you believe are great leaders and describe why you believe each is a leader. Send that person an e-mail expressing what you admire about his or her leadership ability and how much you appreciate his or her influence. Ask if you can conduct an interview to learn more about how that person became a strong leader. You may conduct the interview via e-mail or in person. You may want to use some of these questions below:

- ★ When did you first realize you were able to positively influence other people?
- ★ During your childhood, what did your parents do that may have influenced your ability to lead?
- ★ What experiences did you have as a child, teenager, or young adult that impacted your ability to lead?
- ★ Who are the great leaders that have inspired you and why?
- ★ What are your favorite books or authors that help you learn more about leadership?

You may want to ask if it is possible to shadow the leader for a day so that you could observe and study him or her in action. Be sure to clear this with your parents first!

NOMINATION FORM FOR THE LEADERS' HALL OF FAME

Think about someone you'd like to nominate for the Leaders' Hall of Fame.

I nominate:

This person was (is) a great leader because:

People will always remember this person for accomplishing:

RIDDLES AND PUZZLES ABOUT GREAT LEADERS

Brainstorm various riddles and puzzles about great leaders and share them with your friends.

Riddles

Puzzles

LEADERSHIP JOURNAL

STYLES OF LEADERSHIP

Research the various styles of leadership and brainstorm the names of leaders who exhibit each style.

Great Autocratic Leaders

Great *Laissez Faire* Leaders

Great Democratic Leaders

LEADERSHIP JOURNAL

PAST LEADERS ON CURRENT ISSUES

Brainstorm a list of past leaders and then brainstorm a list of current issues. Match any past leader to a current issue and discuss how you think he or she may have responded to it.

Past Leaders	Current Issues

LEADERSHIP JOURNAL

GREAT LEADERS MATRIX

Using books, journals, and online resources to gather information about great leaders of the past and present, complete the Leadership Matrix by writing names in the blanks. Be sure to include female and male leaders, as well as those from different ethnic and religious backgrounds.

Leaders in . . .	International	National	State	Community/Regional
Business/Industry				
Education				
Government				
Humanities				
Mathematics				

GREAT LEADERS MATRIX, CONTINUED

Leaders in . . .	International	National	State	Community/Regional
Medicine				
Performing Arts				
Politics				
Religion				
Science/Technology				
Sports				

Chapter 7
Journal Entries

Advice to Others

LEADERSHIP POSITIONS THAT I WOULD LIKE TO HAVE IN THE FUTURE

Brainstorm a list of leadership positions that you would like to have and include the anticipated years by which you anticipate reaching these goals.

School Position	Year

Community Position	Year

Religious Position	Year

ADVICE FROM GREAT LEADERS

Choose five great leaders and develop a skit based on the advice each would give. You'll need stage props, costumes, and students for roles. Select an audience to which you will present your skit.

Great Leaders	Advice

LEADERSHIP JOURNAL

TELEVISION COMMERCIAL SCRIPT

Develop a 60-second TV commercial to encourage younger students to become leaders. In planning the commercial, think of the most important message, words, colors, pictures, and music you want to use to capture peoples' attention. Sixty seconds is not long at all! Time your script out precisely. You could use computer animation for the commercial or videotape real people. Post it on YouTube, and after getting permission from your teacher, show it to your classmates. Make it creative and fun!

Message about leadership:

Words that represent leadership:

Colors that represent leadership:

Pictures, photographs, or visual representations of leadership:

Music that represents leadership:

LEADERSHIP WEB SITE

Develop a leadership Web site for young people, making it as interactive as possible. To get ideas, research some of the leadership Web sites given in the Resources section of this book. Sketch out the components you want to include. For example, you might want to use a purpose statement, a resource section for posting interesting information about leaders and leadership, a section for blogging about leadership experiences, and the like. You may make it as simple or complex as your skills in technology allow. Get help from your technology teacher at school when you reach the development phase.

LEADERSHIP JOURNAL

Leadership
Action Forms

SAMPLE E-MAIL TO OBTAIN MORE INFORMATION

Dear (Ms., Mrs., Mr., or Dr.) Leadership,

I am very interested in getting involved with your organization and would like more information. Please send me any brochures, pamphlets, Web links, or other materials on your organization and any other resources that may be available relating to (topic).

I appreciate your attention to my request, and I look forward to getting involved with (name of organization)!

Sincerely,
(Name)

LEADERSHIP ACTION FORMS

CONTACT LOG

Person (Title, Address, Number, E-Mail)	Reason	Result

INTERVIEWS

Interviewer:

School/Club:

Purpose:

Person Interviewed:

Title:

Organization:

Address:

E-mail:

Date: _____   Time: _____

Questions:

Responses:

L
E
A
D
E
R
S
H
I
P

A
C
T
I
O
N

F
O
R
M
S

THANK YOU LETTER

(Ms., Mrs., Mr., or Dr.) Janet/Joe Leadership
100 Leadership Drive
Leader, Leadership 00000

Dear (Ms., Mrs., Mr., or Dr.) Leadership:

Thank you for your help with _____. The time you spent _____ for _____ made a
(organization name)
great impact because _____. Our _____ was a huge success and we could not have done it without your help.

We appreciate your time and effort. Your assistance will always be remembered.

Sincerely,

(Name)

LEADERSHIP
DEVELOPMENT PLAN

My goal:

Objectives:

Activities:

Resources/People:

Timeline:

Other:

LEADERSHIP ACTION FORMS

SURVEYS

A survey may take many forms with several response modes. Two examples are yes or no; and strongly agree (SA), agree (A), disagree (D), undecided (U), or don't know (DK). In addition, open-ended responses also are used. However, open-ended responses are difficult to tally and people often are more likely to complete a survey if they are not required to write a response. Develop a survey on leadership to give to others. Tally the results and share them with your classmates.

Item	SA A D U DK Yes No

LEADERSHIP ACTION FORMS

TALLY RESULTS

	SA	A	D	U	DK		Yes	No
Item 1						or		
Item 2								
Item 3								
Item 4								
Item 5								

Results and Conclusions:

PETITION FORM

Title:

Group or Association:

Purpose:

We would like to initiate or change the following:

The following students agree to the above.

Name	E-Mail Address	Phone	Date

Be sure to check about the number of signatures required.

NEWS RELEASE

A news release should be concisely written and contain only the most important information. Be sure to be accurate in facts and names. Like other stories, a news release should give details including who, what, where, when, why, and conclusions.

For Immediate Release

LEADERSHIP ACTION FORMS

❑ Newspaper   ❑ TV   ❑ Radio

Name of Contact Person:

Contact Information:

Leadership Quotes

Leadership is not a property of the individual but a complex relationship among all the variables.
   —*John McGregor*

You cannot be a leader, and ask other people to follow you, unless you know how to follow, too.
   —*Sam Rayburn*

Remember that the best and purest form of leadership is example; that "Come on" is a much better command than "Go on."
   —*Queen Elizabeth II*

Management is doing things right; leadership is doing the right things.
   —*Peter F. Drucker*

A leader is a dealer in hope.
   —*Napoleon Bonaparte*

The very essence of leadership is that you have to have a vision. You can't blow an uncertain trumpet.
   —*Theodore M. Hesburgh*

You gain strength, courage and confidence by every experience in which you really stop to look fear in the face. You must do the thing you think you cannot do.
   —*Eleanor Roosevelt*

The real leader has no need to lead—he is content to point the way.
   —*Henry Miller*

Leadership consists not in degrees of technique but in traits of character; it requires moral rather than athletic or intellectual effort, and it imposes on both leader and follower alike the burdens of self-restraint.
   —*Lewis H. Lapham*

The quality of a person's life is in direct proportion to their commitment to excellence, regardless of their chosen field of endeavor.
   —*Vincent T. Lombardi*

No man will make a great leader who wants to do it all himself, or to get all the credit for doing it.
   —*Andrew Carnegie*

Leadership is practiced not so much in words as in attitude and in actions.
—*Harold Geneen*

The quality of a leader is reflected in the standards they set for themselves.
—*Ray Kroc*

A leader must have the courage to act against an expert's advice.
—*James Callaghan*

The key to successful leadership today is influence, not authority.
—*Kenneth Blanchard*

A leader takes people where they want to go. A great leader takes people where they don't necessarily want to go, but ought to be.
—*Rosalynn Carter*

Leadership should be more participative than directive, more enabling than performing.
—*Mary D. Poole*

Leadership is a combination of strategy and character. If you must be without one, be without the strategy.
—*General H. Norman Schwarzkopf*

If your actions inspire others to dream more, learn more, do more, and become more, you are a leader.
—*John Quincy Adams*

Men make history and not the other way around. In periods where there is no leadership, society stands still. Progress occurs when courageous, skillful leaders seize the opportunity to change things for the better.
—*Harry S. Truman*

I don't know the key to success, but the key to failure is trying to please everybody.
—*Bill Cosby*

If you really want something, work hard, take advantage of opportunities, and never give up, you will find a way.
—*Jane Goodall*

I skate where the puck is going to be, not where it has been.
—*Wayne Gretzky*

If you want the rainbow, you have to put up with the rain.
—*Dolly Parton*

As long as you are going to be thinking anyway, think big.
—*Donald Trump*

People make things happen. All the rest is just window dressing.
—*Oprah Winfrey*

The art of leadership is saying no, not yes. It is very easy to say yes.
—*Tony Blair*

The function of leadership is to produce more leaders, not more followers.
—*Ralph Nader*

It is the responsibility of intellectuals to speak the truth and expose lies.
—*Noam Chomsky*

Outstanding leaders go out of their way to boost the self-esteem of their personnel. If people believe in themselves, it's amazing what they can accomplish.
—*Sam Walton*

Leadership and learning are indispensable to each other.
—*John F. Kennedy*

As we look ahead into the next century, leaders will be those who empower others.
—*Bill Gates*

I am personally convinced that one person can be a change catalyst, a "transformer" in any situation, any organization. Such an individual is yeast that can leaven an entire loaf. It requires vision, initiative, patience, respect, persistence, courage, and faith to be a transforming leader.
—*Stephen R. Covey*

Great leaders are almost always great simplifiers, who can cut through argument, debate, and doubt to offer a solution everybody can understand.
—*General Colin Powell*

Lead and inspire people. Don't try to manage and manipulate people. Inventories can be managed, but people must be led.
—Ross Perot

In choosing a president, we really don't choose a Republican or Democrat, a conservative or liberal. We choose a leader.
—Rudy Giuliani

There are many qualities that make a great leader. But having strong beliefs, being able to stick with them through popular and unpopular times, is the most important characteristic of a great leader.
—Rudy Giuliani

Somebody has to take responsibility for being a leader.
—Toni Morrison

Never neglect details. When everyone's mind is dulled or distracted the leader must be doubly vigilant.
—General Colin Powell

Leaders need to be optimists. Their vision is beyond the present.
—Rudy Giuliani

To lead people, walk beside them.
—Lao Tzu

One measure of leadership is the caliber of people who choose to follow you.
—Dennis A. Peer

Remember the difference between a boss and a leader;
a boss says, "Go!" A leader says, "Let's go!"
—*E. M. Kelly*

A man who wants to lead the orchestra must turn his back
on the crowd.
—*Max Lucado*

Nearly all men can stand adversity, but if you want to
test a man's character, give him power.
—*Abraham Lincoln*

The final test of a leader is that he leaves behind him in
other men the conviction and the will to carry on.
—*Walter Lippmann*

Leadership is the special quality which enables people to
stand up and pull the rest of us over the horizon.
—*James L. Fisher*

A frightened captain makes a frightened crew.
—*Lister Sinclair*

Nothing is so potent as the silent influence of a good
example.
—*James Kent*

If I, the group leader, expect you, the group member, to be
weak, then I elicit the weak part of you. If I expect you to
be able to cope, I elicit your strength.
—*Will Schutz*

Never doubt that a small group of thoughtful, committed citizens can change the world. Indeed, it's the only thing that ever has.

—*Margaret Mead*

Resources

LEADERSHIP BOOKS FOR YOUTH

Bouani, J. (2006). *Tyler & his solve-a-matic machine.* **Atlanta: Bouje.**
(Ages 9–12)

In this clever and entertaining story, 10-year-old Tyler builds a machine that will help him get his homework done. The solve-a-matic, though, does much more than that for Tyler. On his journey, he meets fascinating people who help him to learn important lessons about how to be successful. This story encourages readers to use their imaginations, be resourceful, work hard, and take risks.

Covey, S. (1998). *The 7 habits of highly effective teens.* **Wichita: Fireside.**
(Ages 13 and up)

This entertaining yet practical book includes cartoons, quotes, clever ideas, and extraordinary true stories about teens overcoming obstacles and making a difference.

Fakharzadeh, C., & Todd, M. (2007). *Student organization leadership: A guide for student leaders.* **San Diego: Aventine Press.**

(Ages 11 and up)

This book is a useful guide for anyone who wants to begin a student group (e.g., club, committee, assembly) in either high school or college. The authors (experienced student leaders themselves) offer structured guidance as well as personal examples and suggestions. Topics include meeting agendas, advertising, electing officers, and more.

Gerhardt, P. (2008). *Leadership Lucy: A leader everyone can learn from.* **Tacoma: Leadership Success.**

(Ages 9–12)

This book teaches business and leadership fundamentals through the story of a wise woman who opens a successful restaurant with her husband. The story illustrates lessons in goal-setting, cooperation, and the like.

Halpin, M. (2004). *It's your world—If you don't like it, change it: Activism for teenagers.* **New York: Simon Pulse.**

(Ages 13 and up)

This book covers issues ranging from war and AIDS to school violence and bullying and offers practical suggestions for making positive change. Inspiring success stories and difficulties are included for each issue.

Hoose, P. (2002). *It's our world, too! Young people who are making a difference: How they do it—How you can, too!* **New York: Farrar, Straus and Giroux.**

(Ages 9–12)

Containing more than a dozen accounts of children who have worked for everything from racial equality to world peace, this book demonstrates how youth have fought for what's right, then offers ideas about how to get involved.

Lay, K. (2004). *Crown me!* **New York: Holiday House.**

(Ages 9–12)

Justin is appointed king of his fifth-grade class, but learns that being the ruler isn't what he expected. The humorous story illustrates what can happen when power is misused and teaches lessons about teamwork.

Lewis, B. (1998). *The kid's guide to social action: How to solve the social problems you choose—And turn creative thinking into positive action.* **Minneapolis, MN: Free Spirit.**

(Ages 9–12)

This easy-to-follow guide helps youth, teachers, and parents to plan their course of social action regarding a wide variety of issues such as toxic waste and youth rights advocacy. A helpful appendix includes forms such as a grant application checklist.

Lewis, B. (2007). *The teen guide to global action: How to connect with others (near & far) to create social change.* **Minneapolis, MN: Free Spirit.**

(Ages 13 and up)

This book is made up of inspiring true stories of young people making a difference on a global scale. It is very user-friendly and includes specific service opportunities and resources.

Macdonald, F. (2001). *Politics, society, and leadership through the ages.* **Lanham, MD: Lorenz Books.**

(Ages 9–12)

This illustrated book educates young readers about leaders from all over the world and from many different periods throughout history.

Maxwell, J. C. (2001). *Leading at school.* **Nashville, TN: Thomas Nelson.**

(Ages 9–12)

This book offers a step-by-step plan for the development of leadership skills for elementary and middle school students. It focuses on peer relationships, influence, priorities, integrity, problem solving, and self-discipline.

Mayer, C. (2007). *Being a leader.* **Portsmouth, NH: Heinemann.**

(Ages 4–8)

The simple text and beautiful illustrations bring timeless lessons to life. Principles include taking turns and sharing, leading by example, and following rules.

Sabin, E. (2004). *The giving book: Open the door to a lifetime of giving.* New York: Watering Can Press.

(Ages 6–11)

This fun and interactive book inspires young readers to consider their hopes and dreams for the world and empowers them to act in ways that will help these dreams be realized.

Sabin, E. (2005). *The hero book: Learning lessons from the people you admire.* New York: Watering Can Press.

(Ages 6–12)

This interactive book helps young readers to recognize which traits they find admirable in other people and empowers them to emulate these characteristics in themselves. Fun conversation starters and activities are included.

Saunders, J., Beebe, R., & Saunders, A. (2006). *Discovering the real me: Student textbook 11: Developing leadership skills.* New York: Universal Peace Federation.

(Ages 16–17)

This book helps youth to develop leadership skills in a variety of areas including relationships, finances, diversity, and the environment. It includes true stories of successful leaders, questions for reflection, and more.

Schuette, S. (2006). *I am a leader.* Mankato, MN: Capstone Press.

(Ages 4–8)

Text and photographs describe different ways of being a leader. A few pages are dedicated to ways of being a leader at school, while another section is related to leadership at home. The book also includes a useful glossary and a list of helpful leadership-oriented Web sites.

Strack, J. (2006). *Leadership rocks: Becoming a student of influence.* Nashville, TN: Thomas Nelson.

(Ages 9–12)

This study guide equips students with knowledge and skills related to leadership. It focuses on moral courage, selflessness, truth, dependability, endurance, enthusiasm, preparation, and other important characteristics and actions.

Waldman, J. (2000). *Teens with the courage to give: Young people who triumphed over tragedy and volunteered to make a difference.* Newburyport, MA: Conari Press.

(Ages 13 and up)

In this book, 30 incredible young people tell their personal stories of overcoming major obstacles and ultimately helping others. Examples include an amputee running in the Paralympics, the son of a cancer patient creating support groups for kids with sick parents, and a girl who helped her mother and younger sister as they died of AIDS and who is now an AIDS awareness and prevention volunteer.

Woyach, R. (1993). *Preparing for leadership: A young adult's guide to leadership skills in a global age.* Westport, CT: Greenwood Press.

(Ages 13 and up)

In this book, Woyach presents his inclusive model of youth leadership. The book will engage teenage readers, but is also a useful resource for guidance counselors, coaches, club supervisors, and others who may serve as advisers to young people.

Zeiler, F. (2006). *A kid's guide to giving.* Norwalk, CT: Innovative Kids.

(Ages 13 and up)

This book inspires young people to contribute to charitable causes and helps them to make informed decisions about which charities to choose and how to contribute.

YOUTH LEADERSHIP WEB SITES

NYLC: National Youth Leadership Council

http://www.nylc.org

The National Youth Leadership Council's mission is to build vital, just communities with young people through service-learning.

HOBY: Hugh O'Brian Youth Leadership

http://www.hoby.org

This organization's mission is to inspire and develop a global community of youth and volunteers to a life dedicated to leadership, service, and innovation.

YLI: Youth Leadership Institute

http://www.yli.org

Youth Leadership Institute (YLI) works with young people and the adults and systems that impact them to build communities that invest in youth.

National Youth Leadership Forum

http://nylf.org

Founded in 1992, the National Youth Leadership Forum (NYLF) is a tuition-based 501 (c)(3) nonprofit educational organization established to help prepare extraordinary young people for their professional careers.

The Points of Light Youth Institute

http://www.pyli.org

This institute encourages youth to begin a lifelong journey of leadership and meaningful community service by equipping them with leadership skills and peer support networks.

National Council on Youth Leadership

http://www.ncyl.org

The purpose of the National Council on Youth Leadership (NCYL) is to recognize and foster high ideals of leadership and integrity among the youth of America.

YLSN: Youth Leadership Support Network

http://www.worldyouth.org

Through diverse leadership and civic engagement opportunities, this training network seeks to prevent violence and promote self-expression, the arts, and education.

The National Youth Leadership Network

http://www.nyln.org

The National Youth Leadership Network (NYLN) is dedicated to advancing the next generation of young leaders with disabilities.

Youthleadership.com

http://www.youthleadership.com

Youthleadership.com is dedicated to providing current, creative, and dynamic youth leadership education information and serving as a resource clearinghouse for individuals who work with youth leaders.

National Teen Leadership Program

http://www.teenleader.org

National Teen Leadership Program (NTLP) is a high-energy program designed to motivate and inspire students to positions of leadership.

The Be a Champion Foundation

http://www.beachampion.org

This foundation seeks to improve community life of underprivileged youth by inspiring them to "Be a Champion" in their interactions with others at school, at home, on the athletic field, and throughout the community.

*Lead*America Youth Leadership Conferences

http://www.lead-america.org

*Lead*America values integrity, self-confidence, personal responsibility, and a sense of purpose. They offer academic, career-focused, and international youth leadership programs for students in grades 6–12.

We Generation: Youth Hub for Global Change

http://we.freethechildren.com

This Web site provides youth with the tools, information, and inspiration they need to make a positive difference through community volunteering and activism.

Do Something

http://www.dosomething.org

Do Something is a jumpstart for teens looking for projects to start, funding, or ways to get involved locally or globally. Potential leadership activities can be sorted by project, location, or interest area.

STUDENT LEADERSHIP ORGANIZATIONS

America's Promise Alliance

1110 Vermont Avenue, N.W., Ste. 900
Washington, DC 20005
http://www.americaspromise.org

America's Promise Alliance seeks to build the character and competence of the nation's youth by encouraging its national partners to expand opportunities for youth programs. It offers a variety of youth-oriented conferences, programs, and leadership opportunities in addition to research and progress reports to its partners.

Anchor Clubs

Pilot International Building
P.O. Box 4844
Macon, GA 31208-4844
http://www.pilotinternational.org/html/anchor/anchor.shtml

Anchor Clubs are service organizations for high school students. Students participate in community service projects and promote public awareness of brain disorders.

Amnesty International Youth Program

5 Penn Plaza
New York, NY 10001
http://www.amnestyusa.org/student-center/page.do?id=1041074

Local groups of students receive information about human rights abuses worldwide. Student groups can register and receive an activist toolkit.

Boy Scouts of America

P.O. Box 152079
Irving, TX 75015-2079
http://www.scouting.org

Boy Scouts is a national network of clubs devoted to developing the character, leadership, citizenship, and fitness of young men through the age of 18.

Boys and Girls Clubs of America

1275 Peachtree Street, NE
Atlanta, GA 30309
http://www.bgca.org

This youth service organization's primary focus is on youth development. Programs and services are available for youth aged 6–18.

Camp Fire Boys and Girls

1100 Walnut Street, Ste. 1900
Kansas City, MO 64106-2197
http://www.campfireusa.org

Camp Fire views itself as "an organization with and of youth, not just for youth." With programs for children of all ages, Camp Fire has a range of opportunities for self-discovery, decision making, and leadership.

Center for Creative Leadership

One Leadership Place
P.O. Box 26300
Greensboro, NC 27438-6300
http://www.ccl.org/leadership/index.aspx

This educational institute offers practical, research-based tools for developing creative leadership potential. Many participants in programs come from business and industry, education, government, and public service backgrounds.

Congressional Youth Leadership Council

1919 Gallows Road, Ste. 700
Vienna, VA 22182
http://www.cylc.org

The Congressional Youth Leadership Council (CYLC) offers educational leadership conferences for outstanding young people from across the country and around the world nominated based on academic achievement. The program is designed to inspire outstanding youth to reach their full leadership potential.

4-H

1400 Independence Ave., S.W., Stop 2225
Washington, DC 20250-2225
http://4-h.org/index.html

A national program for youth ages 9–19. Local activities vary, but the general emphasis is on leadership development, competition, public speaking, and awareness of natural resources.

EXCEL Clubs

National Exchange Club
3050 Central Ave.
Toledo, OH 43606-1700
http://www.nationalexchangeclub.org/programofservice/Youth/ExcelClubs.htm

Excel Clubs are high school community service clubs that are dedicated to responsible citizenship and service. Students work to improve their school, communities, and country through volunteerism.

Future Business Leaders of America

1912 Association Drive
Reston, VA 20191-1591
http://www.fbla-pbl.org

FBLA is an organization for middle school, high school, and college students who are planning business careers. Chapters are generally run as school clubs.

Future Problem Solving Program International

2015 Grant Place
Melbourne, Fl 32901
http://www.fpspi.org

The Future Problem Solving Program is a program for students of all ages who are involved in gifted and talented programs. Teams of students from all over the world compete in problem-solving contests that address issues of the future.

Gavel Club

Toastmasters International
23182 Arroyo Vista

Rancho Santa Margarita, CA 92688
http://www.gavelclub.org

Sponsored by Toastmasters International, the adult organization devoted to better public speaking, Gavel Club offers opportunities for students to study and participate in speech making and quality public speaking.

Girl Scouts of the USA

420 Fifth Avenue
New York, NY 10018-2798
http://www.girlscouts.org

Through Girl Scouting programs, girls ages 5–17 learn about personal development, decision making, life skills, community spirit, and leadership. Activities range from local meetings to camps and international conferences.

Hugh O'Brian Youth Foundation

31255 Cedar Valley Drive, Ste. 327
Westlake Village, CA 91362
http://www.hoby.org

High school sophomores who are nominated by their schools may attend local, regional, and national seminars on leadership. This foundation encourages youth to live a life dedicated to leadership, service, and innovation.

INROADS

10 S. Broadway, Ste. 300
St. Louis, MO 63102
http://www.inroads.org

INROADS trains and places minority youth in business opportunities. Its mission is "to develop and place talented minority youth in business and industry and prepare them for corporate and community leadership."

Interact

Rotary International
One Rotary Center
1560 Sherman Avenue
Evanston, IL 60201

http://www.rotary.org/en/studentsandyouth/youthprograms/interact/pages/
ridefault.aspx

Sponsored by local rotary clubs, the high school level Interact Clubs are devoted to service, personal responsibility, and integrity, and to the development of leadership skills.

Junior Civitan International

P.O. Box 130744
Birmingham, AL 35213
http://www.civitan.com/index.php?t=jr

Junior Civitan is a community service club for junior and senior high school students. The clubs usually concentrate on helping persons who are disabled and raising funds to support this cause.

Junior Optimist Octagon International

4494 Lindell Boulevard
St. Louis, MO 63108
http://www.optimist.org/e/member/JOOI1.cfm

For all grade levels, these clubs encourage youth involvement in the community. The organization is dedicated to self-improvement through service to the community and awareness of civic affairs.

Junior State of America

400 South El Camino Real, Ste. 300
San Mateo, CA 94402
http://www.jsa.org

The Junior State of America is a student-run organization with chapters nationwide. It fosters direct student involvement in the processes of government through numerous debates, mock government programs, and other activities.

Key Club International

3636 Woodview Trace
Indianapolis, IN 46268-3196
http://slp.kiwanis.org/KeyClub/home.aspx

Key Club is a service organization for high school students that teaches leadership through serving others. It is the world's largest high school service organization.

KidsFACE

P.O. Box 158254
Nashville, TN 37215
http://www.kidsface.org

Individual members and groups create environmental programs within their own communities and keep in touch with other student activists nationwide. Membership is open to students ages 9 and up.

Learning to Lead

P.O. Box 1046
Kennett Square, PA 19348
http://learningtolead.org

Learning to Lead exists to educate, create, enhance, and develop leadership skills in others so that through this education, these emerging leaders can make a positive impact in their schools and/or communities.

National Association of Student Councils

1904 Association Drive
Reston, VA 20191-1537
http://www.nasc.us/s_nasc/index.asp

This organization promotes student governments, improves communication between students and teachers, and gives guidance for student government programs.

National Youth Leadership Council

1667 Snelling Avenue North, Ste. D300
St. Paul, MN 55108
http://www.nylc.org

The National Youth Leadership Council (NYLC) has a variety of programs and publications to help individuals and groups of young people in developing leadership skills.

Odyssey of the Mind

c/o Creative Competitions Inc.
406 Ganttown Road

Sewell, NJ 08080

http://www.odysseyofthemind.com

Odyssey of the Mind is an educational program that encourages the development of creative thinking and problem-solving skills for students from kindergarten through high school.

Outward Bound

100 Mystery Point Rd.

Garrison, NY 10524

http://www.outwardbound.org

Outward Bound wilderness adventure trips provide opportunities for personal growth in leadership ability and self-esteem. Trips are available in various locations and involve different types of outdoor activities.

Project Service Leadership

12703 NW 20th Ave.

Vancouver, WA 98685

http://www.projectserviceleadership.org

This organization helps schools and communities establish service learning in the schools at all levels.

Serteen

1912 E. Meyer Blvd.

Kansas City, MO 64132

http://www.sertoma.org/Page.aspx?pid=272

Serteen is a service organization for students ages 11–19. Clubs raise funds for specific needs in their communities and do service projects to benefit their communities as well.

Sierra Student Coalition

408 C St., NE

Washington, DC 20002

http://ssc.sierraclub.org

Sierra Club's Environmental Youth Leadership Training will help create future environmental and community leaders by introducing, inspiring, and educating youth, especially underrepresented minorities, about the significant and contemporary environmental issues facing their local communities.

YMCA Teen Leadership Programs

101 N. Wacker Drive
Chicago, IL 60606
http://www.ymca.net/programs/programs_for_teens.html

Based on the idea that each generation must have a direct understanding of democracy, the program uses model government activities and debate opportunities to develop leadership skills in young people.

Youth for Understanding International Exchange

6400 Goldsboro Road, Ste. 100
Bethesda, MD 20817
http://www.yfu.org

Youth for Understanding International Exchange (YFU) is a private, nonprofit organization dedicated to international understanding and world peace through its cultural exchange program. It offers year, semester, and summer exchange opportunities for high school students.

Youth Leaders International

1000 Parrs Ridge Dr.
Spencerville, MD 20868
http://www.leaders.org

Youth Leaders International is a modern, vibrant, and fun organization for today's youth and tomorrow's leaders that provides leadership training and programming through mentoring, life skills, and service projects.

Youth Leadership Training 3000

Brooks & Brooks Foundation Inc.
6320 Canoga Ave., Ste. 1500
Woodland Hills, CA 91367
http://www.youthleadership3000.org

The program was inspired by the Brooks & Brooks Foundation to create balance and stability for students through leadership training. The program teaches students about goal setting, money management, community service, how to prepare for college, and more.

References

Gardner, H. (1999). *Intelligence reframed: Multiple intelligences for the 21st century.* New York: Basic Books.

Goleman, D. (1995). *Emotional intelligence: Why it can matter more than IQ.* New York: Bantam Books.

Goodwin, D. K. (2008, September 14). The secrets of America's great presidents. *Parade Magazine.* Retrieved from http://www.parade.com/articles/editions/2008/edition_09-14-2008/2President_Secrets

Hersey, P., & Blanchard, K. H. (1982). Leadership style: Attitudes and behaviors. *Training and Development Journal, 36(5),* 50–52.

Lee, R. J., & King, S. N. (2001). *Discovering the leader in you: A guide to realizing your personal leadership potential.* San Francisco: Jossey-Bass.

Leslie, J. (2003). *Leadership skills and emotional intelligence.* Greensboro, NC: Center for Creative Leadership.

Maxwell, J. C. (2002). *Leadership 101: What every leader needs to know.* Nashville, TN: Thomas Nelson.

Partnership for 21st Century Learning. (n.d.). *Framework for 21st century learning.* Retrieved June 26, 2009, from http://www.21stcenturyskills.org/index.php?Itemid=120&id=254&option=com_content&task=view

Pink, D. H. (2006). *A whole new mind: Why right-brainers will rule the world.* New York: The Penguin Group.

About the Authors

Frances Karnes is professor and director of the Frances A. Karnes Center for Gifted Studies at the University of Southern Mississippi (USM). She also directs the Leadership Studies Program and is widely known for her research, innovative programs, and leadership training. She is author or coauthor of more than 200 published papers and is coauthor of 49 books and has three new books in production. Her work is often cited as the authority on gifted children and the law. She is extensively involved in university activities and civic and professional organizations in the community. Her honors include: Faculty Research Award, Honorary Doctorate from Quincy University, Mississippi Legislature Award for Academic Excellence in Higher Education, USM Professional Service Award, USM Basic Research Award, Rotary International Jean Harris Award, Woman of Achievement Award from the Hattiesburg Women's Forum, Distinguished Alumni Award from the University of Illinois, and Lifetime Innovation Award from the University of Southern Mississippi. The Board of Trustees of Mississippi Institutions of Higher

Learning honored her by naming the research, instructional, and service center she founded at USM the Frances A. Karnes Center for Gifted Studies.

Suzanne M. Bean is director of the Roger F. Wicker Center for Creative Learning and professor of education at Mississippi University for Women (MUW). For the past 27 years, she has served in the field of gifted studies as a teacher of gifted students, director of the Mississippi Governor's School, and founder and director of various other programs for gifted students and their teachers and parents. She has served as director of graduate studies and coordinator of graduate programs in education at MUW. Dr. Bean has coauthored seven books, including *Methods and Materials for Teaching the Gifted* (3rd ed.), and has had numerous publications in professional journals. She also has coauthored numerous grants and she was the lead author of the grant that established the Roger F. Wicker Center for Creative Learning. For the past two decades, she has made numerous presentations at the state, regional, and national levels. She served as president of the Mississippi Association for Gifted Children (formerly MATAG), and she is currently serving as chairperson for the advisory board of that organization. Her dissertation and continued research has been in the area of developing leadership potential in children and adults.